The Effective Teacher's Guide to Sensory Impairment and Physical Disability

Teachers need to be equipped with informed and practical strategies for educating children with sensory impairment and physical disability.

The Effective Teacher's Guide to Sensory Impairment and Physical Disability clarifies the definitions of visual, hearing and multi-sensory impairment. The book also discusses physical disabilities, and examines medical conditions that may lead to the requirement of SEN provision, including epilepsy, spina bifida and cerebral palsy. Writing in an accessible style, the author looks at ways of dealing with a variety of conditions, always with practical classroom situations in mind. In each section the book:

- sets out the definitions of the condition
- explains the legal contexts
- looks at the range of provision
- suggests intervention and support strategies

Highly accessible and authoritative, this book provides teachers with an invaluable source of useful information that will help them to create a responsive classroom.

Michael Farrell is an independent educational consultant and recognised expert in special education. He has written or edited over 30 acclaimed education books.

New Directions in Special Educational Needs

By focusing firmly on what really works in practice with children with special educational needs, this highly practical series will enlighten and inform any busy teacher eager to know more about individual difficulties, and who wants to make inclusion a reality for their pupils.

All books in the series concentrate on the educational implications of certain special educational needs. They also consider the legal obligations of schools, what teachers can do to support and encourage inclusive learning in their classroom, and where they can go for additional support and advice. Packed full of down-to-earth yet authoritative advice, this series will provide teachers with everything they need to ensure their pupils with special needs are effectively and properly supported.

Titles in the Series (all by Michael Farrell)

The Effective Teacher's Guide to Behavioural, Emotional and Social Difficulties
Practical strategies

The Effective Teacher's Guide to Autism and Communication Difficulties
Practical strategies

The Effective Teacher's Guide to Dyslexia and Other Specific Learning Difficulties
Practical strategies

The Effective Teacher's Guide to Moderate, Severe and Profound Learning Difficulties
Practical strategies

The Effective Teacher's Guide to Sensory Impairment and Physical Disability
Practical strategies

The Effective Teacher's Guide to Sensory Impairment and Physical Disability

Practical strategies

Michael Farrell

Routledge
Taylor & Francis Group

LONDON AND NEW YORK

First published 2006
by Routledge
2 Park Square, Milton Park, Abingdon, Oxon OX14 4RN

Simultaneously published in the USA and Canada
by Routledge
270 Madison Ave, New York, NY 10016

Routledge is an imprint of the Taylor & Francis Group

© 2006 Michael Farrell

Typeset in Times New Roman and Gill by
Florence Production Ltd, Stoodleigh, Devon
Printed and bound in Great Britain by
Bell & Bain Ltd, Glasgow

British Library Cataloguing in Publication Data
A catalogue record for this book is available from the British Library

Library of Congress Cataloging in Publication Data
A catalog record has been requested for this book

ISBN10: 0–415–36042–0

ISBN13: 9–78–0–415–36042–5

Contents

Abbreviations

BECTA	British Educational Communications and Technology Agency
BSL	British Sign Language
CMV	cytomegalovirus
DAHISS	Deaf And Hearing Impairment Support Services
DARTs	Directed Activities Related to Text
DELTA	Deaf Education Through Listening and Talking
DfEE	Department for Education and Employment
DfES	Department for Education and Skills
GCSE	General Certificate of Secondary Education
ICT	information and communications technology
ILAE	International League Against Epilepsy
LEA	local education authority
MDVI	multiple disabilities and visual impairment
MOVE	Movement Opportunities Via Education
OME	otitis media with effusion (glue ear)
PLASC	Pupil Level Annual School Census
PMLD	profound and multiple learning difficulties
PSHCE	personal, social, health and citizenship education
PSHE	personal, social and health education
QCA	Qualifications and Curriculum Authority
RNIB	Royal National Institute for the Blind

RNID   Royal National Institute for the Deaf

SE   signed English

SEN   special educational needs

SENCO   special educational needs co-ordinator

SLD   severe learning difficulties

STM   short-term memory

TC   total communication

WHO   World Health Organization

Acknowledgements

I am very grateful to the following colleagues for their kind help: Eileen Boothroyd, Sense, for providing information and suggesting contacts; Dr Stuart Aitken, Senior Research Fellow at the University of Edinburgh, for commenting on a draft of the chapter on deafblindness; Robert Saggers, Royal National Institute for the Blind Research Library, and Angela Edwards, RNIB, for supplying and confirming information for the chapter on visual impairment; and Chris Stevens, Head of SEN and Inclusion, British Educational Technology Association, for providing information on the use of information and communications technology for deaf children for the chapter on hearing impairment.

Dr Michael Farrell trained as a teacher and as a psychologist at the Institute of Psychiatry and has worked as a head teacher, a lecturer at the Institute of Education, London and as a local education authority inspector. He managed national projects for City University and for the Government Department of Education. Michael Farrell presently works as a special educational consultant. This has involved policy development and training with LEAs, work with voluntary organisations, support to schools in the independent and maintained sectors, and advice to ministries abroad. Among his numerous books, which are translated into European and Asian languages, are:

Key Issues for Primary Schools (Routledge, 1999)

Key Issues for Secondary Schools (Routledge, 2001)

Understanding Special Educational Needs: A Guide for Student Teachers (Routledge, 2003)

Key Issues in Special Education (Routledge, 2005)

Chapter 1

What are sensory impairments and physical disabilities?

INTRODUCTION

This chapter sets the book in the context of the 'New Directions in Special Educational Needs' series of which it forms a part. It outlines the contents of the book and describes the proposed readers. I then explain the nature of sensory impairments and of physical disabilities and describe pupils considered to have these impairments or disabilities. This is done with reference to the *Special Educational Needs Code of Practice* (DfES, 2001a); the guidance, *Data Collection by Type of Special Educational Needs* (DfES, 2003); and the legal definition of special educational needs (SEN). An outline of the information received through the senses is provided. The sort of provision from which pupils with sensory impairments and physical disabilities appear to benefit is touched on.

Later chapters consider the causes of particular sensory impairments and of particular physical disabilities and look at the factors associated with these as well as their prevalence. In the present chapter the issue of inclusion is examined with particular reference to pupils with sensory impairments and physical disabilities. I look at the balance of pupils in mainstream and special schools in the context of the guidance, *Inclusive Schooling: Children with Special Educational Needs* (DfES, 2001b). Finally, the chapter examines the issues of multi-professional working, working with parents and involving pupils.

The place of this book in the New Directions in Special Educational Needs series and an outline of the chapter contents

This book, *The Effective Teacher's Guide to Sensory Impairments and Physical Disability: Practical Strategies*, is part of a 'New Directions in Special Educational Needs' series covering the types of SEN related to those outlined in the *Special Educational Needs Code of Practice* (DfES, 2001a). The series focuses on what works in the education of pupils with SEN. It covers:

- behavioural, emotional and social difficulties;
- learning difficulties (moderate, severe, and profound and multiple learning difficulties);

- ◆ specific learning difficulties (dyslexia, dyspraxia and dyscalculia);
- ◆ communication and interaction difficulties (speech, language and communication difficulties, and autistic spectrum disorder);
- ◆ sensory and physical difficulties (visual impairment, hearing impairment, multi-sensory impairment and physical disability).

The present book concerns:

Chapter 2: Visual impairment

This defines visual impairment, low vision and blindness and examines estimates of the prevalence of visual impairment. The chapter looks at some of the developmental implications of visual impairment. I outline some causes of visual impairment and give examples of types of visual impairment. Identification and assessment are considered with regard to the assessment of vision and assessment for education. Provision is discussed with reference to such factors as low vision devices, Braille and hands-on experiences.

Chapter 3: Hearing impairment

This chapter examines definitions of hearing impairment and deafness and the prevalence of these conditions. The causes of hearing impairment and its implications are discussed. Identification and assessment are considered with reference to the assessment of hearing and to educational assessment. Educational provision is explained, with particular attention to communication, literacy and mathematics.

Chapter 4: Provision for deafblind children

This chapter defines deafblindness, outlines some of its causes, considers its prevalence and examines its implications according to whether hearing impairment and/or visual impairment are congenital/early onset or are acquired. I look at provision for pupils who are deafblind with particular attention to communication and (more briefly) gaining information about the world and mobility.

Chapter 5: Physical and motor disability, and medical conditions

This chapter concerns the educational implications of physical disabilities. I consider the medical conditions of spina bifida and hydrocephalus, muscular dystrophy and cerebral palsy. The chapter then examines the educational implications of spinal curvatures and limb loss or damage. I consider cystic fibrosis, epilepsy, diabetes and asthma. With regard to each of these conditions, I seek to define the condition and consider its causes and symptoms. The chapter focuses on educational implications, particularly as they relate to the physical and motor aspects of the conditions.

Chapter 6: Conclusion

The final chapter draws together some common themes of previous chapters.

Each chapter has its own introduction and headed sections and ends with thinking points and key texts. At the end of the book are a list of physical and internet addresses, a bibliography and a combined subject and author index.

Proposed readers

The book is intended particularly for the following readers:

◆ all teachers, special educational needs co-ordinators (SENCOs) and head teachers in mainstream schools and units working with pupils with sensory impairments and physical disabilities;
◆ all staff in special schools providing for pupils with sensory impairments and physical disabilities;
◆ local education authority (LEA) officers with an interest in and/or responsibility for pupils with sensory impairments and physical disabilities;
◆ student teachers and newly qualified teachers wishing to gain an understanding of educational provision for pupils with sensory impairments and physical disabilities;
◆ teachers and others undergoing continuing professional development;
◆ school advisers and inspectors.

What are sensory impairments and physical disabilities?

The Special Educational Needs Code of Practice

As a starting point, the *Special Educational Needs Code of Practice* (DfES, 2001a) provides a basic description of 'sensory and/or physical needs'. It states that:

> There is a wide spectrum of sensory, multi-sensory and physical difficulties. The sensory range extends from profound and permanent deafness or visual impairment through to lesser levels of loss, which may be only temporary. Physical impairments may arise from physical, neurological or metabolic causes that only require appropriate access to educational facilities and equipment; others may lead to more complex learning and social needs; a few children will have multi-sensory difficulties some with associated physical difficulties. For some children the inability to take part fully in school life causes significant emotional stress or physical fatigue.
>
> (DfES, 2001a, Chapter 7: section 62)

Possible triggers for intervention at the level of Early Years Action include 'the practitioner's or parent's concern about a child who, despite receiving appropriate educational experiences . . . has sensory or physical problems, and continues to make little or no progress despite the provision of personal aids and equipment' (4: 21). In the case of Early Years Action Plus in general, the triggers for seeking help outside the school could be that, 'despite receiving an individualised programme and/or concentrated support, the child . . . has sensory or physical needs, and requires additional equipment or regular visits for direct intervention or advice by practitioners from a specialist service' (4: 31).

In the primary phase, the triggers for School Action could be 'the teacher's or others' concern, underpinned by evidence, about a child, who despite receiving differentiated learning opportunities: . . . has sensory or physical problems, and continues to make little or no progress despite the provision of specialist equipment' (5: 44). School Action Plus triggers in the primary phase could be that 'despite receiving an individualised programme and/or concentrated support under School Action, the child . . . has sensory or physical needs, and requires additional specialist equipment or regular advice or visits by a specialist service' (5: 56).

Turning to the secondary sector, School Action triggers (6: 51) and School Action Plus triggers (6: 64) are almost identical to those for the primary phase.

Regarding the statutory assessment of SEN, when an LEA is deciding whether to carry out an assessment, it should consider evidence of attainment and other forms of assessment and 'seek evidence of any other identifiable factors that could impact on learning outcomes' (7: 43). The *Code* does not include in its examples of the latter specific reference to sensory and physical difficulties.

The guidance, Data Collection by Type of Special Educational Needs

A further description of sensory impairments and physical disabilities is provided in the guidance, *Data Collection by Type of Special Educational Needs*, which is connected with the Pupil Level Annual School Census (PLASC) (DfES, 2003) (www.dfes.gov.uk/sen). The Department for Education and Skills (DfES) sent original draft descriptions to a sample of schools, LEAs and voluntary organisations and amended them in the light of the comments received. The guidance describes separately visual impairment, hearing impairment, multi-sensory impairment and physical disability. Schools are required only to record the types of need for pupils where special educational provision is being made at Early Years Action Plus, School Action Plus or through a statement of SEN.

Concerning visual impairment it is stated that it:

> refers to a range of difficulties from minor impairment through to blindness. Pupils with visual impairments cover the whole ability range. For educational purposes, a pupil is considered to be visually impaired if they require adaptations to their environment or specific differentiation of learning materials in order to access the curriculum.
>
> (p. 6)

Pupils are only recorded if additional provision is being made to help them access the curriculum. Regarding blindness, the guidance states that:

> Pupils who are blind or have very limited useful sight require tactile methods of learning, such as Braille and 3-D representations, together with making optimal use of their hearing. Partially sighted pupils also need differentiated materials and may use enlarged print or a mix of learning methods.
>
> (p. 6)

Regarding hearing impairment, it is stated that:

> Pupils with hearing impairment range from those with mild hearing loss to those who are profoundly deaf. They cover the whole ability range. For educational purposes, pupils are regarded as having a hearing impairment if they require hearing aids, adaptations to their environment and/or particular teaching strategies in order to access the concepts and language of the curriculum.
>
> (p. 6)

As is the case for pupils with visual impairment, pupils with hearing impairment should only be recorded if additional educational provision is being made to help them access the curriculum. A number of pupils with hearing impairment, it is noted, 'also have an additional disability or learning difficulty' (p. 6)

Turning to multi-sensory impairment, pupils should only be recorded as having MSI if 'their sensory impairment is their greatest need' (p. 7). The guidance states:

> Pupils with a multi-sensory impairment have a combination of visual and hearing difficulties. They are sometimes referred to as deafblind but may have some residual sight and/or hearing. Many also have additional disabilities but their complex needs mean that it may be difficult to ascertain their intellectual abilities. . . . Pupils with multi-sensory impairments have much greater difficulties in accessing the curriculum and the environment than those with a single sensory impairment. They have difficulties in perception, communication and in the acquisition of information. Incidental learning is limited. The combination can result in high anxiety and multi-sensory deprivation. Pupils need teaching approaches, which make good use of their residual hearing and vision, together with their other senses. They may need alternative means of communication.
>
> (DfES, 2003, p. 7)

With reference to physical disability, the guidance indicates:

> There is a wide range of physical disabilities and pupils cover the whole ability range. Some pupils are able to access the curriculum and learn effectively without additional educational provision. They have a disability but do not have a special educational need. For others, the impact on their education may be severe. In the same way, a medical diagnosis does not necessarily mean that a pupil has SEN. It depends on the impact the condition has on their educational needs. . . . There are a number of medical conditions associated with physical disability, which can impact on mobility. These include cerebral palsy, heart disease, spina bifida, hydrocephalus, and muscular dystrophy. Pupils with physical disabilities may also have sensory impairments, neurological problems or learning difficulties. Some pupils are mobile but have significant fine motor difficulties which require support. Others may need augmentative or alternative communication aids.
>
> (DfES, 2003, p. 7)

Sensory impairments and physical disabilities and the legal definition of SEN

Many types of SEN can be better understood by examining them in the context of the legal definition of SEN in the Education Act 1996. The Act provides a layered definition in which a 'difficulty in learning' or a 'disability' may lead to a 'learning difficulty', which may call for special educational provision to be made, therefore constituting an SEN.

It has already been stated that visual impairment may be 'minor' and that hearing impairment may be a 'mild hearing loss'. To the extent that these impairments are severe enough to lead to a 'learning difficulty' that calls for special educational provision to be made, they are considered to be an SEN. Multi-sensory impairment is by definition severe and is therefore regarded as a learning difficulty constituting an SEN. Regarding physical disability, it has already been pointed out that some children have a disability but do not have a special educational need.

Only where the disability gives rise to a learning difficulty calling for special educational provision to be made is it considered to be an SEN.

Information received through the senses

Even a brief outline of the information that is received through the senses can indicate how much is taken for granted when the senses are unimpaired. The sense of touch gives information on such qualities as hardness and softness, texture, shape, pliability, weight, hollowness or solidity, and atmosphere (dry, steamy, cold, warm).

The sense of smell provides information helping one to recognise such materials and items as leather, wood, metal, paint, flowers and, more generally, whether a smell is acrid or sweet. Taste includes information such as sweetness, sourness and saltiness.

The so-called 'distance senses' of sight and hearing also provide a wealth of information. Sight indicates colour, tone, contrast, perspective, depth, size, shape, opaqueness or transparency, reflection, light intensity and duration and enables the use of television, visual print, photographs and so on. Hearing gives information relating to pitch, volume and timbre, allowing one to recognise such phenomena as the human voice, the rustling of grass, household and school sounds, traffic, music, animal sounds and the sea.

Proprioceptive sense conveys information about body position and the position of the limbs and head, muscle position, direction, balance, movement, stillness, weight, acceleration and deceleration.

Provision for pupils with sensory impairments and physical disabilities

Later chapters of the book separately explore provision for pupils with visual impairment, those with hearing impairment, pupils who are deafblind, those with physical disabilities and learners with certain medical conditions. The present section indicates something more about the nature of sensory impairments and physical disabilities by touching on the interventions that are used when educating pupils with sensory impairments and physical disabilities. As a starting point, the *Special Educational Needs Code of Practice* (DfES, 2001a) provides a basic description of provision from which pupils with sensory impairments and physical disabilities may benefit. They may require some or all of the following:

◆ appropriate seating, acoustic conditioning and lighting;
◆ adaptations to the physical environment of the school;
◆ adaptations to school policies and procedures;
◆ access to alternative or augmented forms of communication;
◆ provision of tactile and kinaesthetic materials;
◆ access to different amplification systems;
◆ access to low vision aids;
◆ access in all areas of the curriculum through specialist aids, equipment or furniture;
◆ regular and frequent access to specialist support.

(DfES, 2001a, 7: 62)

The guidance, *Data Collection by Type of Special Educational Needs*, connected with the PLASC (DfES, 2003) (www.dfes.gov.uk/sen) indicates that pupils should only be recorded with reference to hearing impairment or visual impairment or physical disability 'if additional educational provision is being made to help them to access the curriculum'. Pupils should only be recorded in terms of multi-sensory impairment if their sensory impairment is their greatest need (pp. 6–7).

Causal factors and prevalence of sensory impairments and physical disabilities

The causal factors associated with, and the prevalence of, sensory impairments and physical disabilities are considered separately for visual impairment, hearing impairment, deafblindness, physical disability and certain medical conditions in subsequent chapters.

Inclusion and pupils with sensory impairments and physical disabilities

One understanding of inclusion is that it aims to encourage a school to reconsider its structure, teaching approaches, pupil grouping and use of support so that the school responds to the perceived needs of all its pupils. Teachers, collaborating closely, seek opportunities to look at new ways of involving all pupils and to draw on experimentation and reflection. There should be planned access to a broad and balanced curriculum developed from its foundations as a curriculum for all pupils.

Inclusion is sometimes viewed as concerning educating more pupils in mainstream schools and fewer or none in special schools and other venues regarded as segregating. However, it may be argued that special schools can also be inclusive (Farrell, 2000). Indeed, the Qualifications and Curriculum Authority (QCA) has characterised inclusion as, 'securing appropriate opportunities for learning, assessment and qualifications to enable the full and effective participation of all pupils in the process of learning' (Wade, 1999).

An aspect of inclusion is that of including pupils with SEN who are already in mainstream schools. This approach seems to be the purpose of documents seeking to encourage this kind of inclusion, such as the *Index for Inclusion* (Booth and Ainscow with Black-Hawkins, 2000). The document concerns the inclusion of all those connected with the school, adults as well as children, not only pupils with SEN. Developing an inclusive ethos and inclusive approaches may increase the school's capacity to include pupils with sensory impairments and physical disabilities who are presently not in mainstream or who otherwise might be considered to be better placed in another setting such as a special school or a unit.

The expression, 'full inclusion', as it applies to pupils with SEN, indicates the view that all pupils with SEN should be educated in mainstream schools. A range of provision such as mainstream school, special school, pupil referral unit or home tuition would not be acceptable. It would be better to have increased support and resources in mainstream schools in proportion to the severity and complexity of SEN (e.g. Gartner and Lipsky, 1989). Full inclusion is not the position of the government in England nor is it that of any of the major parties in opposition at the time of writing.

The document, *Inclusive Schooling: Children with Special Educational Needs* (DfES, 2001b), gives statutory guidance on the framework for inclusion. The Special Educational Needs and Disability Act 2001 is said to deliver a 'strengthened right to a mainstream education for children with special educational needs' (p. 1, paragraph 4) by amending the Education Act 1996.

Concerning the nature of the proposed 'right' to inclusion, it is clear that this is constrained. This is indicated by the *Inclusive Schooling* document referring to a 'strengthened right' to mainstream education (p. 1, para. 4). The right (if that is the correct word) is partial. The extent of the right can be seen from the commensurate duties that are placed on others in connection with the 'right'.

As a result of the Special Educational Needs and Disability Act 2001, the Education Act 1996 section 316(3) was amended to read:

> If a statement is maintained under section 324 for the child, he must be educated in a mainstream school unless that is incompatible with:
>
> ◆ the wishes of his parent, or
> ◆ the provision of efficient education for other children.

The use of the word 'must' in the above section of the Act indicates the duty of the LEA and others that corresponds to the 'right' to be educated in the mainstream. If the education of a child with SEN is incompatible with the efficient education of other pupils, mainstream education can only be refused if there are no reasonable steps that can be taken to prevent the incompatibility. But it may not be possible to take steps to prevent a child's inclusion being incompatible with the efficient education of others. This may arise, for example, where the teacher, even with other support, has to spend a greatly disproportionate amount of time with the child in relation to the rest of the class.

The 'rights' are further affected when one considers a particular school rather than the generic concept of 'mainstream'. A parent may express a preference for a particular mainstream school to be named in their child's statement of SEN. In this case, schedule 27 of the Education Act 1996 requires the LEA to name the parents' preferred choice of school in the child's statement unless any of three conditions apply. These are:

1 the school cannot provide for the needs of the child;
2 the child's inclusion at the school would be incompatible with the efficient education of other pupils;
3 the child's inclusion at the school would be incompatible with the efficient use of resources.

It will be seen that there is no comprehensive 'right' of attendance at a mainstream school, but that the rights of the parents of a child with SEN are balanced against the 'rights' of the parents of children who do not have SEN and against other factors.

Professionals working closely together

Professionals involved with children with sensory impairments and physical disabilities may include the teacher; specialist teachers for the blind, the deaf and the deafblind; audiologist; optometrist; general practitioner; school nurse; school medical officer; LEA advisory staff; educational psychologist; social worker; and others. Each may have different professional perspectives and different levels of experience concerning sensory impairments and physical disabilities. Professional trust is essential but is difficult to build up where staff turnover is very high. For multi-professional working to be practicable, clear lines of communication are necessary and a structure that demarcates responsibility without being too constraining.

Early years development and childcare partnerships use inter-agency planning to bring together early years education and social care. Health action zones and education action zones co-ordinate action on social disadvantage and social support for pupils with SEN. SEN regional partnerships have encouraged discussions and joint planning between education, health and social services on some topics. Aspects of the Excellence in Cities programme included encouraging school-based learning support units working with pupils at risk of exclusion from school to engage with learning mentors and out-of-school support services. The Sure Start initiative offered the opportunity to interrelate family policy and the early identification and support of pupils with SEN.

In 2003, an Early Support Pilot Programme was designed to develop good service provision and to assist development in various areas including the co-ordination of multi-agency support for families and partnership across agencies and geographical boundaries. This involved joint work between the DfES and others, including the Royal National Institute for the Blind (RNIB), the Royal National Institute for the Deaf (RNID), and the National Children's Bureau (www.earlysupport.org.uk). See also the DfES website (www.dfes.gov.uk/sen), the Department of Health website (www.doh.gov.uk) or the National Children's Bureau website (www.ncb.org.uk).

Related to joint professional working, a National Children's Trust Framework was announced in 2001 intended to develop new standards across the National

Health Service and social services for children and to encourage partnership between agencies. Children's Trusts were subsequently seen as seeking to integrate local education, social care and some health services (through the Health Act 1999 section 31) for children and young people and to incorporate an integrated commissioning strategy. The LEA will include potentially all education functions, including SEN, the education welfare service and educational psychology. Children's social services will include assessment and services for children 'in need'. Community and acute health services will include locally provided and commissioned child and adolescent mental health services and could also include speech and language therapy, health visiting and occupational therapy services concerned with children and families. (Primary Care Trusts will be able to delegate functions to the Children's Trust and will be able to pool funds with the local authority.)

Children's Trusts can also include other services such as Connexions, Youth Offending teams and Sure Start. Other local partners such as the police, voluntary organisations, housing services and leisure services can be involved. Children's Trusts are expected to sit within local authorities reporting to the director of children's services, who in turn will report through the chief executive to the local councillors. The Children's Trusts will commission services and may provide these directly or by contracts through public, private or voluntary sector organisations.

The resulting integration of service provision is expected to be reflected in such features as: collocated services such as Children's Centres and extended schools; multi-disciplinary teams and a key worker system; a common assessment framework across services; information-sharing systems across services; joint training; and effective arrangements for safeguarding children. The intention is to integrate key children's services within a single organisational focus, preferably through Children's Trusts, which it was envisaged would exist in most areas by 2006. Bids for 35 'Pathfinder' Trusts were approved in 2003, funded to 2006 (www.doh. gov.uk/nsf/children/index.htm).

Working with parents

Working closely with parents is an aspiration of all schools and a continuing theme in government guidance. The *Special Educational Needs Code of Practice* (DfES, 2001a) devotes a chapter to 'Working in partnership with parents' and specific guidance on seeking to understand what parents need is available (e.g. Greenwood, 2002). The school's support of parents may include:

♦ providing information about SEN and practical strategies for coping;
♦ putting parents in touch with support groups locally and nationally;
♦ making school premises available for various activities such as a parents support group;
♦ having displays of literature such as leaflets;
♦ being a 'one stop' point of contact for other services.

A model for collaborating with parents in order to help pupils experiencing difficulties at school is suggested by Hornby (2003, p. 131), which may have wider application for work with parents of pupils with SEN more generally. It distinguishes between what it is thought parents 'need' and what it can reasonably be expected they can contribute.

Parents *needs* are considered to be for communication with the school (which all parents need); liaison, such as that taking place at parent–teacher meetings (which most parents need); education, such as parents' workshops (which many need); and support, such as counselling (which some need).

Parents' *contributions* are considered as information, for example about the child's strengths (which all parents can provide); collaboration, for example with behaviour programmes or supporting a pupil's individual education plans (to which most parents could contribute); resources, such as being a classroom aid (which many could contribute); and helping develop policy, for example being a parent governor of the school (which some could contribute).

The model leaves open the exact interpretation of what the expressions 'most', 'many' and 'some' might mean and schools will bring their own judgements to bear on, for example, whether it is reasonable to expect 'many' parents to contribute at a level suggested by being a classroom aid. Nevertheless the basic structure of the model with a graduated view of the parents' proposed needs and the contribution is a helpful one.

Pupils' views

Materials used when seeking to explore the views of children with learning difficulties include such sources as: the guidelines, *Listening to Children with Communication Support Needs* (Aitken and Millar, 2002) and *How It Is* (Marchant and Cross, 2002); and projects such as *Can You Hear Us?: Including the Views of Disabled Children and Young People* (Whittles, 1998*)*. Lewis (2004) lists some aspects of methods relevant to chronologically young children or 'developmentally young' children. These include:

- permit or encourage 'don't know' responses and requests for clarification;
- stress not knowing the events or views of the child to counter the child's assumption that the adult knows the answer (the child tends to be more suggestible if the adult has credibility and rapport with the child);
- use statements rather than questions to trigger fuller responses from children;
- if using questions, use an appropriate level of generality (for example 'open or moderately focused questions seem to generate more accurate responses from children with learning difficulties than do highly specific questions');
- avoid 'yes/no' questions to avoid acquiescence, particularly for pupils with learning difficulties; and
- aim for an uninterrupted narrative.

(Lewis, 2004, pp. 4–6 paraphrased)

The *Special Educational Needs Code of Practice* (DfES, 2001a, especially Chapter 3) encourages pupil participation and seeks to involve pupils with sensory impairments and physical disabilities in the development and evaluations of the individual education plan and behaviour support plans where applicable. A balance is sought between encouraging participation and overburdening the pupil when he may not have sufficient experience and knowledge to make judgements without support.

THINKING POINT

Readers may wish to consider with reference to particular school:

◆   the effectiveness of procedures for seeking a commonly held understanding of sensory impairments and physical disabilities such as discussion, consultation with the SENCO, and observation.

KEY TEXT

Farrell, M. (2003) *The Special Education Handbook*, London, David Fulton Publishers.

As a starting point, entries that may be useful include: disability, impairment, audiology, audiologist, health visitor, birth difficulties, cerebral palsy, chromosome abnormalities, dual sensory impairment, epilepsy, genetic disorders, hearing impairment, medical conditions, motor impairment, physical disability, visual impairment, adaptive equipment, aids to hearing, Braille, sign language and total communication (TC). Appendices on legislation, related reports and consultative documents; regulations; and circulars and circular letters include summaries of circulars relating to the education of sick children (*Circular 12/94*) and supporting pupils with medical needs in schools (*Circular 14/96*).

Chapter 2

Visual impairment

INTRODUCTION

This chapter defines the terms 'visual impairment', 'blindness' and 'low vision', and examines development implications of visual impairment. I consider estimates of the prevalence of visual impairment. The chapter outlines some causes of visual impairment and gives examples of types of visual impairment such as errors of refraction. Identification and assessment are considered with regard to the assessment of vision and assessment for education (although the two are of course related). Provision is then discussed with reference to such factors as low vision devices, Braille and hands-on experiences. The chapter concludes with a consideration of visual impairment and multiple disability.

Definitions of visual impairment, blindness and low vision

In this chapter, the term 'visual impairment' is used to indicate a continuum of loss of sight and includes blindness unless otherwise specified. Where blindness is referred to specifically, it is intended to describe the level of sight loss of children who depend mainly on tactile methods of learning. The expression 'low vision' is used with reference to children whose learning and teaching mainly involve methods relying on sight.

Some developmental implications of visual impairment

Visual impairment affects social and emotional development, language development, cognitive development and mobility and orientation. The combination of these effects on development influences the functioning and learning potential of a child with visual impairment. Strategies are necessary to minimise the potentially adverse effects of visual impairment. For example, regarding social and emotional development, in a local playgroup a child with visual impairment who is unable to see what other children are doing may not be invited to join in. The adult in charge may need to encourage and stage-manage co-operation (e.g. Kingsley, 1997, p. 24).

The development of the preschool child with visual impairment is discussed by Stone (1997a), who raises issues to do with emotional and social development, motor development, language development, and the growth of independence skills, possible behaviour difficulties and other matters.

Before a child with visual impairment starts primary school, the teacher for the visually impaired will usually provide the school with details of assessments of the child's vision and the educational implications. A mobility officer or the teacher will help the child find his way around the new school. Careful consideration will be given to the classroom environment so that such factors as the illumination, the use of tactile displays with Braille labelling and the print resources being used all enable the pupil's learning.

During adolescence, there are implications relating to visual impairment and physical, cognitive, social and emotional developments. For example, regarding the physical and sexual changes of adolescence, a fully sighted person can see these developments and compare them to similar changes experienced by peers. But an adolescent with visual impairment cannot see these changes and has to rely mainly on verbal descriptions, while touching taboos constrain the opportunity to explore bodily changes in others (Kirkwood, 1997, p. 111). Challenges also arise in the transition to adulthood, in further and higher education, and in preparing for and following a career.

Prevalence of visual impairment

Prevalence in relation to SEN refers to the number of children with a particular type of SEN in a specified population over a specified period, for example 0 to 5 years old or school age. Incidence is usually expressed as the number of children per live births in a given year. Prevalence is related to incidence in that prevalence is determined by the incidence of a condition and its duration (see also Farrell, 2003, pp. 129–30).

From returns relating to a survey by the RNIB, reported in 2003, involving a sample of education services for people with visual impairments in LEAs, it was estimated that 20,870 children up to the age of 16 years in England experienced visual impairment (Keil and Clunies-Ross, 2003). This indicated a prevalence rate of 2.5 per 10,000 children in England (p. 13). Of these children, 30 per cent had additional 'complex needs', including severe learning difficulties (SLD) or profound and multiple learning difficulties (PMLD) (p. 15). Only 1.4 per cent of the children in the survey were deafblind. The great majority of pupils with visual impairment who read and write use print, while about 4 per cent of children and young people aged 5 to 16 years use Braille as the main medium for learning (p. 28).

Regarding 'visual impairment', in January 2004 in England (DfES, 2004, table 9), there were 2,970 pupils at School Action Plus representing 0.8 per cent of pupils at this part of the SEN framework and a further 4,200 with statements of SEN or 1.8 per cent of pupils with statements. The specific figures for ordinary primary and secondary schools and for special schools are as follows. In primary schools, 1,940 pupils with visual impairment were at School Action Plus (0.9 per cent of all pupils at School Action Plus in primary schools) and 1,580 had statements of SEN (2.3 per cent of all pupils with statements in primary schools). In secondary schools, the number was 1,020 at School Action Plus (0.8 per cent) and 1,630 with statements of SEN (2.1 per cent). In special schools, where it is much less usual for pupils *not* to have statements of SEN, there were only 10 pupils at School Action Plus (0.5 per cent) and 990 with statements of SEN (1.1 per cent). The figures for special schools included pupils attending maintained and non-maintained special schools but excluded pupils in independent special schools and pupils in maintained hospital schools.

Causes and types of visual impairment

Causes of visual impairment may involve factors that are genetic; that arise during foetal development or during the birth process; or that occur in childhood. Various conditions and syndromes, some of which are genetically determined, can be passed to the child by a parent or both parents who may be unaware that they 'carry' the condition. The availability of genetic counselling enables parents carrying such conditions to plan for children with this information available to them. Factors affecting the development of the foetus or affecting the baby during the process of birth can cause visual impairment. For example, maternal rubella can lead to a baby having visual impairment such as cataracts (where the lens of the eye is cloudy or opalescent resulting in a loss of vision for detail) or microphthalmia (underdeveloped eyes). Where a baby is born prematurely with a birth weight of less than 1,300 grams and where high quantities of oxygen are needed to keep the baby alive, retinopathy of prematurity (damage to the developing retina) sometimes occurs. Neurological disorders can lead to visual pathway damage and cortical visual impairment. This is a visual loss, which may be temporary or permanent, caused by a disturbance of the posterior visual pathways and/or the occipital lobes. The damage to the brain that causes this may occur before, during or after birth, or may be the result of disease or injury. While the eyes may seem normal, visual messages to the brain are not correctly interpreted or acted upon. In childhood, causes of visual impairment include viral infections, brain tumours and injury.

Among types of visual impairment are refractive errors (myopia or short-sightedness, hypermetropia or long-sightedness, and astigmatism) and other types, such as cataract, nystagmus and retinitis pigmentosa.

Refractive errors are often straightforward and corrected by spectacles or contact lenses worn for specified purposes. A child is considered to have visual impairment only if the best corrected vision is significantly outside the normal range for near and distance visual acuity (clarity or sharpness of vision).

In myopia or short-sightedness the eyeball is too long so that parallel light rays coming from a distance do not focus on the retina at the point where they should (the central point of the macula – the fovea). Instead, the light rays are focused between the lens and the macula so distance vision is blurred. Corrective concave spectacles or contact lenses are used.

Hypermetropia or long-sightedness is a condition in which the eyeball is too short and light rays focus behind the retina so that vision is blurred or in extreme cases not effective. In straightforward instances, convex lens spectacles or contact lenses can correct hypermetropia so that light rays are focused on the fovea. However, when other conditions also occur, such as cataracts, visual acuity is reduced even when prescribed spectacles are worn. For children with hypermetropia, long periods of time spent on 'close' tasks such as reading should be avoided because they cause discomfort. Low vision devices such as a closed circuit television may be prescribed for some pupils.

In astigmatism, the main cause is that the lens or the cornea of the eye has irregularities in its curvature that lead to its refractive power being variable, causing the image on the macula to be distorted. A cylindrical correction built into the lens of spectacles can rectify this. But where astigmatism is accompanied by myopia or hypermetropia, correcting vision can result in visual acuity being reduced.

Turning to other types of visual impairment, retinopathy of prematurity and cortical visual impairment have already been mentioned. Further examples are cataract, nystagmus and retinitis pigmentosa.

A cataract is an opaqueness or cloudiness of the lens of the eye preventing some light rays passing to the retina. The school must have advice from an ophthalmologist or an optometrist because a suitable response depends on such factors as the position of the cataract. For example, if the cataract affects the lens periphery, the child will need increased levels of illumination, while, if the centre of the lens is opaque, low lighting will aid vision.

Nystagmus is a repetitive rhythmic involuntary movement of the eyes often accompanied by other visual impairments such as congenital cataracts. A child with nystagmus will have considerable difficulty fixing the eyes on a specified point, although some children can be helped to find an eye position in which involuntary movement is reduced. Line markers for reading and the use of reading materials with bold, well-contrasted print are helpful.

Retinitis pigmentosa refers to a group of progressive conditions affecting the retina, in particular the peripheral area that contains cells (rods) sensitive to vision in dim light. This leads to night blindness and so-called tunnel vision. As retinitis pigmentosa is usually progressive, for some children, eventually, loss of sight is expected so that provision for using Braille and mobility training should be part of the curriculum.

Identification and assessment

Identification

Most severe visual problems are identified within the first few months of the baby's life, perhaps by the maternity hospital, health visitor or parents. Some difficulties may not be appreciated until the child starts school.

Assessment

This sub-section looks at assessments of vision and at educational assessments although of course the two are related. It gives examples of the assessment tools that are used.

Assessment of vision

When a child is very young or unable to co-operate verbally, methods can be used to gain information about vision such as testing blinking reflex or measuring the electrical responses of the visual cortex. A full assessment of vision would be expected to include the following (from Mason *et al.*, 1997, p. 53):

1   a distance vision test;
2   a near vision test;
3   a field of vision test;
4   a test of colour perception;
5   a contrast sensitivity test;
6   an assessment of visual functioning.

For tests 1 to 3 above, each eye is normally tested independently, then both eyes are tested together. Distance vision and near vision are usually tested with and without aids such as spectacles that the child might use. Examples of each type of test 1 to 6 will now be considered.

Distance vision is commonly tested using the Snellen test chart, comprising letters, numbers or pictures arranged in rows of descending smallness. Assuming that letters are used, each row of letters is designed to be recognised at a certain distance by a person with normal vision, for example at 60, 36, 24, 18, 12, 9, 6 or 5 metres. If a child stands 6 metres from a chart and is able to read all the letters down to the row typically read at 6 metres, the child's vision is said to be 6/6. Should they only be able to read to the row typically read from 18 metres while standing 6 metres away, their visual acuity is 6/18. If a child is unable to read the top line of the chart (typically readable at 60 metres) from 6 metres away, vision is less than 6/60 and the test is continued at a shorter distance. If the child can read the top line from 3 metres away, 3/60 is recorded and, if the child can read it from only a metre away, visual acuity is 1/60. The World Health Organization (WHO) classification of visual acuity (WHO, 1980), which is still current, is that 6/6 to 6/18 represents 'normal vision', worse than 6/18 but better than or equal to 3/60 represents 'low vision', and worse than 3/60 represents 'blind'.

Near vision acuity (important for close work such as reading and writing) may be assessed by an 'N print' test involving print of different sizes. Each print size is given an N number so that the larger the N number the larger the print. N5 is the smallest print size. For the test, the print size is recorded along with the distance in centimetres from which it is read, for example N6 at 25 centimetres. Alternatives for young children include tests using pictures graded for size. A child with visual impairment may use very large print size.

The field of vision is the area that a person sees from all parts of the eye when looking directly ahead. Any field of vision defect is mapped out on a circular chart representing the field of vision in each eye.

A well-known test of colour perception is the Ishihara Test, which comprises plates of coloured dots among some of which are numbers or symbols. A person with normal colour vision can distinguish the symbols or numbers, while someone with a loss of colour vision will either not be able to distinguish them or will interpret them incorrectly.

Problems with contrast sensitivity are indicated by a poor response to medium and low frequencies in a contrast sensitivity test. A child with such difficulties will be unable to read easily unless illumination is good and print is very dark against a white background.

Visual functioning concerns how well a child makes use of vision in day-to-day activities. When two children have the same visual acuity they may differ in visual functioning; for example, one child may be more willing to use the vision he has and benefit from better mobility and orientation skills than the other. A qualified teacher of the visually impaired normally makes an assessment of visual functioning, which involves consulting the child and others who know him. The assessment investigates strengths and weaknesses in the way that the child uses vision, taking into account cognitive and social development.

Educational assessments

The *Look and Think Checklist* (Chapman *et al.*, 1989) is a criterion-referenced assessment enabling the teacher to assess a sample of perceptual and cognitive skills of children aged 5 to 11 years. Its 18 sub-scales are intended to assess: discrimination among and identification of two-dimensional and three-dimensional objects; eye–hand co-ordination skills; and colour differentiation abilities. It aims to help the teacher find out what the child can do in the classroom so the teacher can devise tasks that will encourage skills such as scanning, discriminating and matching.

The *British Ability Scales* (Elliot, 2005) has 23 sub-scales, some of which are considered suitable to use with children who are blind or have low vision, for example similarities, word definitions and recall of digits sub-tests, which are presented orally and require an oral response. A tactile version of the speed of information sub-test has been developed and standardised on a blind population (Hull and Mason, 1993).

The *Neale Analysis of Reading Ability (Braille Version)* assesses reading speed, accuracy and comprehension, while parallel forms allow for retesting. It has been standardised for use with blind children (Greaney *et al.*, 1994).

Vision for Doing (Aitken and Buultjens, 1992) aims to assess the functional vision of children with visual impairment and multiple disabilities. It provides an assessment and also indicates how children can be assisted to develop and use functional vision for increasing their understanding of aspects of their physical and social surroundings such as objects and events.

Provision

Professional standards and the role of the specialist teacher

Professional standards for 'additional specialist skills'

While it confirms that the three existing mandatory qualifications for teaching pupils with hearing, visual and multi-sensory impairments remain in force for the 'foreseeable future', the *National Special Educational Needs Specialist Standards*

(Teacher Training Agency, 1999, p. 3) sets out standards concerning the effective teaching of pupils having severe and/or complex needs. These are for use as an auditing tool to help head teachers and teachers identify training and development needs. They are structured as core standards, extension standards, standards in relation to key SEN roles and responsibilities, and skills and attributes. The 'extension standards' give an indication of the knowledge and understanding and the skills associated with teaching children who have a visual impairment. Teachers with additional specialist skills should be able to demonstrate that they know and understand:

> i. the principles underlying the development of alternative and augmented communication systems, including Braille; and their appropriate application in providing a curriculum that utilises pupils' strengths;
> ii. the needs of pupils where English is not the first language, particularly in relation to the effects of cultural inhibitors, *e.g. the different interpretations of signs and gestures*;
> iii. the anatomy and physiology of visual functions in the development of communication;
> iv. the principles of haptic perception.
> (Teacher Training Agency, p. 16, italics in original)

> i. the educational implications of the pathology and treatment of eye diseases and conditions;
> ii. the principles of assessment of functional vision and how appropriate communication strategies can enhance functional vision.
> (p. 25)

Teachers with additional specialist skills should have skills in:

> i. using and developing scales and/or orientation and mobility checklists to assess the needs of pupils;
> ii. using materials designed to evaluate and enhance residual vision;
> iii. employing appropriate techniques for teaching Braille.
> (p. 18)

> i. checking and maintaining low vision devices.
> (p. 26)

The specialist teacher

A specialist teacher for the visually impaired may work in a special school or nursery (LEA, non-maintained or independent), in a specially resourced unit or centre in a mainstream school or as an advisory teacher visiting and working in special and mainstream settings. A specialist teacher working mainly in a special school may be very well placed to provide services elsewhere if the service is properly funded and if the staffing of the special school is enhanced to allow such work as outreach, in-reach, training and consultancy. Joint work with families and schools perhaps drawing on a systems view of provision may be offered.

A visiting specialist teacher for pupils with visual impairment may:

◆ provide advice on the physical environment including lighting and contrast in the environment;
◆ give help in providing the sensory curriculum;
◆ suggest modifications to classroom materials enabling them to be used by pupils who are blind or who have low vision;
◆ give advice on the presentation of activities and specialised teaching strategies.

(Griffiths and Best, 1996)

It has been further suggested that a specialist teacher may contribute to:

◆ the assessment and development of pupils' vision;
◆ the development of movement and mobility skills;
◆ providing staff with an understanding of the nature of visual impairment and its effects on learning.

(Best, 1997, p. 383)

Other contributions include:

◆ providing staff training and contributing to professional development through consultancy;
◆ providing fact sheets, articles, books, charts, posters, videos, CD-ROMs, physical and internet addresses, and other sources of reference;
◆ arranging and facilitating visits to other schools, units and centres;
◆ directly teaching (for example Braille or mobility).

Low vision devices and lighting

The most suitable low vision devices for a child's requirements are determined through consultation involving various people, including the child, parents, an optometrist, a teacher of the visually impaired and a rehabilitation officer. Devices include reading stands, correct illumination, spectacles and magnification equipment.

Ways of achieving magnification include: increasing the size of the image of the object; decreasing the working distance to the object; and increasing the visual angle, for example by using a telescope or other multi-lens device. Devices include a hand magnifier; a stand magnifier; a flat bed magnifier (with a plane base in contact with the surface to be viewed and a hemispheric plano-convex top); a line magnifier; spectacle mounted devices; telescopic devices and closed circuit television (a television camera mounted on a moveable table and connected to a video display monitor). Filter lenses are used for medical conditions in which light impairs vision and reduces visual acuity (for example, cataracts or cone dysfunctions).

Important in relation to pupils with visual impairment are ambient lighting around the school and task lighting to maximise the use of a pupil's near vision while studying. Glare-free lighting should be ensured. Artificial and natural lighting are controlled to ensure that the level of lighting is suitable for particular areas of the classroom. The type of visual impairment influences suitable illumination; for example, pupils who have photophobia require reduced lighting, while other pupils will prefer higher levels of illumination. Blinds, louvres and tinted glass control natural light, while dimmer switches are used to adjust artificial ambient lighting.

Orientation and mobility

Orientation and mobility are two abilities associated with independent movement and travel. Orientation involves being aware of space and where one is within it (Where am I? Where do I want to go? How do I get there?). Mobility is the ability to move around safely. To travel safely, children may use a sighted guide or a long cane. Young adults may also use a guide dog or an electronic aid. Mobility specialists teach more complex skills such as travelling using a long cane in a town. The aim of a mobility programme is to 'progress along the continuum of understanding, control and independence' (Stone, 1997b, p. 162). It is difficult to overstate the importance of orientation and mobility, given their contribution to improving physical fitness, raising self-esteem, providing opportunities to socialise, and increasing the ability to travel to and from a place of employment and so on.

The layout of a school and other features can aid orientation and mobility. A tactile or large print plan of the school in the reception area can help the pupil build up a notion of both the general layout of the school and particular routes to be followed. This would be supplemented by mobility training. Safety is improved by such means as recessed radiators and the use of surfaces that reduce glare on floors. Specific adaptations are necessary for particular subjects of the curriculum. For example, in design and technology, where machinery is used, it must be well defined by colour and lighting. DfES *Building Bulletins*, updated from time to time, are a source of technical guidance.

Tactile representation and hands-on experience

The word 'tactile' is sometimes reserved for a passive touch, such as that of clothing on the body or the sensation on the legs and back associated with sitting on a chair. The terms 'tactual' and 'haptic' are then used to refer to a more active use of touch, such as that involved when exploring the qualities of an object or material and recognising qualities such as temperature, texture, shape, weight and so on. Tactile representations include maps, diagrams, graphs, charts, pictures and mathematical constructions, and may be supplemented by labels and instructions in Braille. Tactile diagrams may use collage (e.g. string, sandpaper, wire, etc.) or 'swell' paper having raised black lines contrasting with a flat white background.

The use and processing of tactile representations and their educational use is subtle. Tactile information is processed sequentially and the 'parts' are used to build up a picture of the whole. When information is processed visually, the whole may be processed and then the detail of the components. For this and other reasons, when the teacher introduces tactile diagrams, she will need to offer explanations and guidance and the pupil will need time to explore the diagram so that it becomes meaningful. For pupils who are fully sighted, the conventions of portraying three-dimensional items or scenes two-dimensionally in photographs or illustrations has to be learned. For the child who uses tactile materials, conveying three-dimensional representations two-dimensionally in tactile form is very difficult, as conventions of perspective, for example, need to be conveyed.

Regarding hands-on experience, in school (and elsewhere) it is important to allow and encourage the pupil with visual impairment to handle materials, objects and artefacts. This can also often be arranged with advance planning in museums, sites of historic interest, art galleries (e.g. sculptures, friezes), farms and so on. In mathematics, for example, hands-on experience is vital in handling money, weighing, measuring, exploring geometrical shapes and making fractional parts.

Gaining rapid and efficient access to information

An important aspect of study skills and a way of gaining greater independence in learning is developing the ability and skills to gain efficient access to information. For example, a tone indexing facility on audiotape recordings or the use of contents summary pages in a Braille book before a lengthier treatment of the subject is read facilitates study. CD-ROMs offer quick access to information through synthesised speech or large character displays. Similarly, it is essential that the pupil has easy access to work he has produced. This includes having a series of easily labelled files for different topics and subjects in which the work is kept on numbered pages and having boxes of computer disks suitably labelled. Using reference materials such as a Braille dictionary is time-consuming and more efficient alternatives for some purposes may be subject-oriented word lists with definitions.

Aspects of oracy and literacy

Listening and speaking

It has been estimated that 80 per cent of the information received by people who are fully sighted comes through the visual mode (Best, 1992). Listening is important in mobility training to help the person with visual impairment to move safely and efficiently (Stone, 1995), for example by listening for sound signals at pedestrian crossings. Listening to curriculum material through such equipment as electronic reading devices, computer programs using synthesised speech, and talking books provides important non-visual information. For example, a variable speed audiotape recorder can be used for higher study to give faster listening speeds and 'compressed speech' devices ensure that the original pitch of the voice is maintained while speaking rate is speeded up.

A classroom with carpeted areas will helpfully reduce unwanted background sounds, allowing the pupil to attend more effectively to relevant sounds. The teacher should speak clearly, remembering that visual clues from her body language may not be available to the pupil with visual impairment. When speaking directly to the pupil, the teacher should use the pupil's name first so that he knows that he is the one being addressed.

Regarding speaking skills, an important aspect for a pupil with visual impairment is learning such skills as looking at the person being addressed when the pupil himself is speaking. Turn-taking skills in conversation and discussion groups are helped by visual clues about body language, which may be unavailable to the pupil with visual impairment, making the interpretation of another person's tone of voice, rhythm of speaking, pauses and other verbal features important clues in timing conversational exchanges.

Reading using tactile methods

Braille uses a 'cell' of six raised dots, combinations of which make up letters, punctuation and contracted words. There are two grades of British Braille. Grade 1 consists of alphabet and punctuation signs and grade 2 contains contractions of words (such as 'RCV' for 'receive'). Early teaching of Braille reading and writing in a special school or a specialist resource centre is usually based on contracted Braille from the beginning. An average reader of Braille reads two or three times more slowly than the average print reader, the respective rates being about 100 words per minute and 250 words per minute (e.g. Aldrich and Parkin, 1989). This is in part because a Braille reader cannot scan ahead in the same way as a sighted reader of print, there being no peripheral touch equivalent to peripheral vision. The reading rate differs in a similar way when children who read print and children who read Braille are compared.

Computer programs can translate print files into Braille files, which are then downloaded to Braille embossers. Moving from print reading to Braille reading for a pupil whose sight is deteriorating requires sensitivity as the pupil may resist Braille reading as an acknowledgement of deteriorating sight. Reading schemes (e.g. ones produced by the RNIB) are available to develop Braille skills for pupils transferring from print to Braille.

Moon is a tactile medium based on a simplified raised line adaptation of the Roman print alphabet. It may be used for pupils with visual impairment and additional difficulties who are unable to learn Braille. Children's reading schemes using Moon are published by the RNIB. A support and advice centre relating to Moon is based at Rushton Hall, an RNIB special school in Northamptonshire (McCall and McLinden, 1996).

Writing in tactile codes and handwriting

Electronic Braillewriters use a six-key format for input, each key corresponding to a dot in the Braille cell. Output may be through synthetic speech or a renewable tactile display on the machine. Text may be stored in the machine's memory to be transferred later to a standard printer or a Braille embosser. Braille text downloaded to a conventional printer is translated by software into print. It is debated whether older pupils should be taught to use dedicated Braille writing devices as the main medium for recording information. The alternative is to teach pupils who are educationally blind to touch type using a conventional QWERTY keyboard in primary school, in order to develop word processing skills early. In secondary school, pupils may use conventional computers with adaptive software and synthesised speech as their main way of writing and storing information.

Moon characters may be written by hand on a plastic material known as german film. Moon fonts have also been developed for computers. Moon text is typed on to the computer screen then downloaded through a conventional printer on to paper. The Moon is then copied onto 'swell' paper and raised by being passed through a stereo-copying machine (McCall, 1997, p. 158).

Turning to handwriting, for a pupil with low vision, this tends to be difficult because the pupil cannot easily see and self-correct work, which may be untidy. Word processing skills may be taught from an early age. For older pupils who are blind, it is important that handwriting is sufficiently developed to sign one's name (Arter *et al.*, 1996).

Personal, social, health and citizenship education (PSHCE)

Self-help skills are best taught in context so that they are meaningful and so that the pupil is motivated to exercise and develop the skill in order to achieve a particular goal. For example, selecting clothing and dressing may be taught to children when it is necessary to change clothes at home at bedtime or at school for physical education lessons.

Day-to-day items can be made easier for pupils with visual impairment to use by making careful choices; for example, dark coloured food such as beef is easier to see on a white plate than on a dark one. Kitchen equipment such as a microwave cooker at home and in school can have tactile controls, labels and instructions. Specialist equipment includes liquid level indicators.

Regarding developing a pupil's increasing independence and autonomy in studying, a balance is sought between offering adult help where necessary and ensuring that the pupil's work is differentiated suitably so that the demands of the task are not excessive. An example is allowing extra time for reading in Braille compared with reading in print for a fully sighted pupil.

Counselling is a broad term encompassing different approaches. In general terms, however, counselling offers the child or young person the opportunity to be listened to. It can help the pupil express feelings in relation to, for example, deteriorating eyesight. It may help in the transition to recognising and accepting when learning Braille and mobility training may be necessary because of deteriorating sight. Counselling can help raise self-esteem, for example by providing a situation in which the child is listened to and given unconditional regard. It can provide an opportunity to talk through any problems and to look at ways they might be resolved.

Information and communications technology (ICT)

Aspects of ICT have already been discussed in earlier sections on 'low vision devices', 'listening and speaking', 'writing in tactile codes' and 'gaining rapid and efficient access to information'. ICT allows a pupil to write an essay by speaking it into a computer. It offers access through sight (e.g. using magnified or large print), hearing (e.g. speech synthesis) and touch (e.g. converting conventional print text into Braille). Information from internet sites is accessed by being downloaded on to a computer then read by a screen reader through speech synthesis, magnification or Braille.

Optical character machines and scanners enable the pupil to read from printed text that is translated into synthesised speech. CD-ROMs having electronic or spoken versions of the same text are replacing talking books, while CD-ROM writers and recorders are now easily available.

Specialist tape recorders used by pupils with visual impairment include multi-track models with speed control, voice indexing facility and control switches with tactile markings. Machines may be desk models or compact ones. A tone indexing facility allows signals to be inserted on to a tape, which can be heard when the tape is fast forwarded or rewound. Some pocket memo recorders are voice activated and also have a tone indexing facility. It will be seen from such examples that ICT can contribute significantly to developing independence in learning.

Access to National Curriculum subjects, extra-curricular activities and accreditation

Aspects of English and of PSHCE have been considered separately and this section examines how access to some other subjects of the curriculum can be aided. In general, concrete experience is important to help the pupil develop concepts, while clear explanations from the teacher and the opportunity for pupils to discuss are vital. Approaches and aids in different subjects illustrate what is done to improve access to the curriculum.

In mathematics, there is a mathematics Braille notation (Braille Authority of the United Kingdom, 1987) and a simplified version (Dorton House School for the Blind, 1995). Also, in music there is an international system of Braille notation. Regarding science, a light-sensitive device such as a light probe allows the pupil to conduct experiments on shadows, reflection and refraction. Equipment such as an electrical thermometer or balance may have a speech output or a large display on a computer screen. History can be enlivened by visits to places of historic interest such as churches, castles and stately homes, 'living' museums and so on. Artefacts in school and elsewhere offer interest and may include old toys, household items, armour or clothing. Similarly, in geography, visits to transport facilities such as canals, rivers, railways and airports and to features such as lakes, rivers, beaches and areas where there are different rock and soil formations can be experienced. Adaptations can be made to physical education equipment, for example by using a ball that contains a bell so that it can be heard. Goalball is a game played in many schools by pupils with visual impairment (Arter and Malin, 1997, p. 286). In art and design, artwork is available through paintings represented using a bas-relief technique with raised edges and an accompanying audiotape (available from the Living Paintings Trust). Raised lines may be drawn using german film. Spur wheels produce raised lines of different heights and textures when drawn across Manila paper.

Extra-curricular activities, including sports, leisure pursuits, clubs, social gatherings and fitness, offer opportunities for the pupil to make contacts and friends in the local community that will continue into adult life. Those running clubs and organising activities who may not have knowledge of visual impairment will need to become conversant with the implications of the particular visual impairment concerned and of such matters as the importance of lighting and the need for good contrast on items such as gymnasium equipment.

In examinations, depending on circumstances, a pupil with visual impairment may use Braille or large print, use a word processor, have a scribe and a reader, and be allowed extra time. Examination papers may be in Braille, large print and modified print or on audiotape. A school may open papers early to check the content.

Visual impairment and multiple disability

An RNIB survey of LEAs gathered data on educational placements of children with visual impairment and with 'multiple disabilities and visual impairment' (MDVI) (Clunies-Ross and Franklin, 1996). This was based on returns from heads of LEA visual impairment services and was intended to establish the ages and distribution of children and young people considered to have multiple disabilities together with information about the criteria used by services to identify the population. This survey indicated that there were 12,679 children aged 5 to 15 years plus with visual impairment and a further 6,691 with MDVI. As McLinden (1997, p. 316) indicates, however, there is vagueness about the term 'multiple disabilities', in part because there are no nationally agreed criteria for it. Some services described pupils as having 'multiple disabilities' if they were educated in a school for pupils with SLD or PMLD. Also, 'vague references' (McLinden, 1997, p. 316) were made to 'learning difficulty' and 'developmental delay'.

An essential aspect of multiple disabilities is the interaction of the disabilities and the combined impact on the child's development. The term has been regarded as meaning the existence of SLD or PMLD with another impairment. For example, Orelove and Sobsey (1991) refer to individuals with severe and profound learning difficulties and 'one or more significant motor or sensory impairments and/or special health care needs'.

Hearing impairment, visual impairment, physical disability and motor difficulties may have been identified by staff in the maternity hospital or by the health visitor or parents. Other difficulties/disabilities such as SLD or speech and language difficulties may be noticed later.

Certain structured assessments are used with children having MDVI and who are at an early level of communication:

◆ *Affective Communication Assessment* (Coupe *et al.*, 1985) is based on structured observation of behaviour made in response to various stimuli at a pre-symbolic level. It enables possible communicative behaviours to be noticed, which can be used to help the pupil develop consistent and suitable communication that can be understood and used by others.

◆ *Assessing Communication Together* (*ACT*) (Bradley, 1991) gives a summary of communication techniques that may be used between a person with sensory impairments and their communication partner, across various communication functions. Augmentative communication methods are covered, such as hand-over-hand signing and objects of reference.

The curriculum for pupils with MDVI comprises a balance between the National Curriculum, including its flexibilities, a developmental curriculum, and additional curriculum provision such as therapies. Flexibility in the National Curriculum includes the use of material from earlier key stages where this is required to enable the pupil's progress and achievement to be demonstrated. Appropriate provision is made for pupils who need to use communication methods other than speech, non-sighted methods of reading, and aids or adapted equipment for writing or for practical activities. A developmental curriculum concerns areas of early development, which may include motor development, communication, cognition and personal/social development. The additional aspects of the curriculum (sometimes called the complementary curriculum) may include mobility education, physiotherapy and movement development programmes such as Movement Opportunities Via Education (MOVE).

Co-ordination is assisted by a cross-curricular approach involving a variety of professionals such as the teacher, mobility officer, speech and language therapist, physiotherapist, occupational therapist and social care worker. Individual education plans with jointly agreed targets and strategies to achieve them can help pull together the shared work of these professionals. Such multi-professional working requires time to enable face-to-face communication, joint planning sessions, and money to pay for the higher staffing levels necessary to create this non-contact time.

For some pupils with MDVI, communication may not be primarily through spoken language or writing. Non-verbal skills may be used, including a manual signing system. Signing such as Makaton may be employed to give visual/gestural support to aid a child's comprehension of spoken language. A switch with a voice output system may be used. Other means of communication may be objects of reference or tactile symbols.

For pupils who are unable to understand and use formal communication systems such as speech or manual signing systems, their potential communication signals may be non-intentional or unconventional. A communication partner may be helpful to seek to relate such signals to meaning. In general terms, a communication partner ensures that stimulation that is structured and suitable is provided in an interactive context. Among characteristics of an effective communication partner (see Porter and Kirkland, 1995) is that they: expect communication; provide opportunities for the child to communicate; encourage attention to communicate and share attention on what the communication is about; seek the communicative meaning of a child's behaviour and respond to it; selectively respond to shape more specific communication attempts; and model the use of language in context through talking about what the child is doing or experiencing. There is some overlap between the provision outlined above and that considered suitable for pupils who are deafblind.

THINKING POINTS

Readers may wish to consider with reference to a particular LEA or school:

◆   whether the LEA offers a range of educational places for pupils with visual impairment, including mainstream school, nursery, specially resourced units, special schools and special nursery;
◆   how effectively training, supervision and liaison with specialist teachers of pupils with visual impairment develop the skills of the non-specialist teacher and enhance the education of pupils with visual impairment.

KEY TEXTS

Mason, H. and McCall, S. with Arter, C., McLinden, M. and Stone, J. (eds) (1997) *Visual Impairment: Access to Education for Children and Young People*, London, David Fulton Publishers.

This book is intended for both parents and professionals who work with children and young people having visual impairment. Various sections cover education, provision and contemporary issues; blindness and low vision (including a chapter on the anatomy and physiology of the eye); and the child and young person with visual impairment (including chapters on 'transition to adulthood', 'careers and vocational education' and 'counselling'). Other sections concern the special curriculum; access to the curriculum; principle of access to the mainstream curriculum (with chapters dealing with particular subjects and extra-curricular activities); children and young people with MDVI; the specialist teacher's role; and teacher education. Some chapters are becoming rather dated and one hopes for a new edition soon.

Keil, S. and Clunies-Ross, L. (2003) *Survey of Educational Provision for Blind and Partially Sighted Children in England, Scotland and Wales in 2002*, London, Royal National Institute of the Blind, Education and Employment Research Department.

As well as providing estimates of the numbers of children up to the age of 16 years who have visual impairment, the survey seeks to establish the type of provision made for their education. There is an indication (worrying if confirmed) that a trend to delegate funds to schools is leading to some LEAs not maintaining an overview of the numbers of children in their area and the provision being made for them.

Chapter 3

Hearing impairment

INTRODUCTION

This chapter examines definitions of hearing impairment and deafness and considers the prevalence of these conditions. The causes of hearing impairment and its implications are examined. Identification and assessment are explained. Several implications of deafness and some issues relating to the education of deaf children are outlined. Educational provision is explained with particular reference to communication, literacy and mathematics. Finally, I consider pupils who are deaf and have disabilities.

Definitions

In order to define hearing impairment and deafness, it is necessary to be clear about the two terms, 'frequency' and 'amplitude/intensity'.

Frequency has to do with the rate at which sound waves vibrate and is usually expressed as cycles per second (c.p.s.). Sound frequency is perceived as pitch; rapidly vibrating sound waves being perceived as high pitched and slowly vibrating sound waves being perceived as low pitched sounds. The human ear is normally responsive to sounds between 60 and 16,000 c.p.s. but is most responsive to sounds between 500 and 4,000 c.p.s. Speech sounds occupy the most responsive band and particular speech sounds involve several frequencies. Vowels tend to occupy the lower frequency range while fricatives, such as 's', 'f', 'th' and 'sh', tend to occupy the higher ones. Hearing loss rarely affects all frequencies equally, so hearing is usually distorted. If there is low frequency loss, the ability to hear vowels is impaired. Should there be higher frequency loss, then the capacity to hear fricatives and sibilants is reduced and, because consonants make speech intelligible, high frequency hearing loss is usually more serious.

Categorisations of hearing impairment relate to intensity/amplitude. The intensity of a sound is experienced as its loudness and is measured in a decibel (dB) scale on which the quietest audible sound is given a value of 0 dB and the loudest sound has a value of 140 dB. Normal speech is about 60 dB. Hearing impairment can be measured on the dB scale in terms of dB loss. The British Association of Teachers of the Deaf recognise four categories of hearing impairment:

(a) slight: not exceeding 40 dB loss;
(b) moderate: a 41 to 70 dB loss;
(c) severe: a 71 to 90 dB loss, and post-lingual loss greater than 95 dB;
(d) profound: at least a 96 dB loss acquired prelingually.

It will be noticed that between severe hearing impairment and profound hearing impairment, a distinction is made between prelingual and post-lingual loss. This distinction is important for future communication. A child who has experience of hearing and using speech may already be speaking and may wish to continue, while a child with a similar loss that occurred before speech developed would be likely to find communication using speech more difficult.

Prevalence

It has been estimated that at a specified time almost 20 per cent of children in the age range 2 to 5 years are affected by otitis media with effusion (see next section), making it a very common disease, although the number of persistent cases is relatively few. Sensori-neural deafness occurs in about 1 in 1,000 babies.

Regarding 'hearing impairment', in January 2004 in England (DfES, 2004, table 9), there were 6,010 pupils at School Action Plus representing 1.7 per cent of pupils at this part of the SEN framework and a further 6,950 pupils with statements of SEN or 2.9 per cent of pupils with statements. The specific figures for ordinary primary and secondary schools and for special schools are as follows. In primary schools, 3,110 of pupils with hearing impairment were at School Action Plus (1.4 per cent of all pupils at School Action Plus in primary schools) and 2,980 had statements of SEN (4.3 per cent of all pupils with statements in primary schools). In secondary schools, the number was 2,840 at School Action Plus (2.2 per cent) and 2,290 with statements of SEN (2.9 per cent). In special schools, where it is much less usual for pupils *not* to have statements of SEN, there were only 50 pupils at School Action Plus (3.2 per cent) and 1,690 with statements of SEN (1.9 per cent). The figures for special schools included pupils attending maintained and non-maintained special schools but excluded pupils in independent special schools and pupils in maintained hospital schools.

Causes of deafness

Deafness may be the result of an ear disease or injury, although profound deafness is usually congenital. In sensory motor deafness, 'sounds' reaching the inner ear are not transmitted to the brain because of damage to the structures within the inner ear or to the acoustic nerve. Defects of the inner ear may be:

◆ congenital because of an inherited fault in a chromosome;
◆ owing to birth injury;
◆ owing to damage to the developing foetus (e.g. because of infection).

The inner ear may also be damaged after birth because of severe jaundice.

Conductive deafness occurs when sound is not properly propagated from the outer ear to the inner ear, usually because of damage to the eardrum or to the bones of the inner ear. Common forms of impaired hearing in children are otitis media (middle ear infection) and otitis media with effusion (OME), sometimes called glue ear, in which sticky fluid collects in the middle ear. Otitis media is the largest cause of hearing loss in children under the age of 12 years (McCracken, 1998a, p. 155). It is treated by the surgical insertion of ventilation tubes ('grommets') into the tympanic membrane to keep the middle ear ventilated; 'watchful waiting' with regular hearing checks and the administration of antibiotics if acute infections occur; or hearing aids.

Identification and assessment

Hearing impairment may be identified through neonatal screening or by the parent, health visitor or later the school through school screening programmes.

The 1982 American Joint Committee on Infant Hearing set out screening risk criteria for congenital or early onset deafness. A summarised version is as follows:

◆ family history of childhood hearing impairment;
◆ congenital perinatal infection;
◆ anatomic malformations involving the head or neck (e.g. cleft palate);
◆ birth weight less than 1,500 grams;
◆ hyperbilirubinaemia at a level exceeding indications for exchange transfusion;
◆ bacterial meningitis, especially due to Haemophilus influenzae;
◆ severe asphyxia.

Habilitation strategies may include hearing aid fitting, counselling and guidance for parents, and the involvement of a teacher of the deaf.

Hearing tests determine whether hearing is impaired, the extent of the impairment, and what part of the ear may be implicated. Audiometry, the measurement of the sense of hearing, often refers to hearing tests using a piece of equipment, an audiometer, to produce sounds of known intensity and pitch. The hearing in each ear is measured in relation to the range of normally audible sounds. Types of test include pure tone audiometry, auditory evoked response and impedance audiometry.

Pure tone audiometry involves the use of an audiometer to produce and measure sounds of different frequency and intensity. The sounds are transmitted through an earphone into one ear while the other ear is prevented from hearing. First the sound is reduced in intensity until it cannot be heard, then the intensity is gradually increased until the person signals that they can detect it.

Auditory evoked response is the brain's response to sound stimulation provided by the audiometer and is analysed using electrodes placed on the scalp. This technique is sometimes used if the child cannot indicate hearing thresholds, for example because he has learning difficulties.

Impedance audiometry is a test used to determine middle ear damage associated with conductive deafness. A probe fitted to the entrance to the outer ear canal emits a continuous sound while air is pumped into the probe. A microphone fitted to the probe detects the differing reflections of sounds from the eardrum as pressure changes in the ear canal, indicating the elasticity of the eardrum and the bones of the middle ear. This indicates the type of disease that is causing the deafness. (For further information on audiology, see Knight and Swanwick, 2002.)

Implications of hearing impairment

Among implications of hearing impairment are those relating to visuo-spatial skills, short-term memory (STM) and cerebral organisation.

Deaf children have demonstrated superior performance on a range of visuo-spatial tasks (e.g. Bellugi *et al.*, 1994). The extent to which this is attributable to sign language enhancing visuo-spatial skills or to deaf infants paying more attention to visual aspects of their surroundings is debated. As McSweeney (1998) observes, there are aspects of visuo-spatial processing at which deaf signers can excel. But, '"spatial cognition" should not be thought of as a single form of processing that is either better or worse in different populations. Rather, different skills are involved' (p. 22).

Studies testing STM, in terms of the order in which items are recalled, indicate that deaf participants recall fewer items than do hearing participants (e.g. Campbell and Wright, 1990). Also, when STM is tested for order in the recall of sign stimuli, deaf participants recall fewer items than hearing signers, which may be owing to hearing signers using a verbal code (which is especially suited to recalling items in order) to remember signs (e.g. Logan *et al.*, 1996). If deaf children derive information from lip reading, which can form the basis of a speech-based code, such a code is probably qualitatively different from the speech-based code used by hearing people (Campbell and Wright, 1990). Variability in the level of speech-based code a deaf child will develop relates to such factors as the degree of hearing loss the child experiences and speech intelligibility. While a possible alternative for deaf signers appears to be an STM code based on the properties of sign language, such a code may take up more memory capacity than speech representations resulting in fewer items being recalled.

Turning to cerebral organisation, hearing people process language predominantly in the left hemisphere, damage to which can lead to language difficulties. Sign language is visually and spatially conveyed and combines the functions of language and visuo-spatial information. A study of three deaf signers having left hemisphere damage showed that they experienced sign language deficits in both expression and comprehension (Poizner and Tallal, 1987). The signer's ability to use gestures and motor skills were unimpaired so the impairment appears to be linguistic, suggesting similarities at the neurological level between the processing of sign language by deaf people and of spoken language by hearing people. But, whereas spoken language can continue with left hemisphere support 'alone', sign language seems to require a contribution from the right hemisphere. Deaf signers with right hemisphere damage had visuo-spatial deficits such as spatial disorientation, just as hearing people would. But their production and comprehension of space used for 'mapping' spatial relations within sign language was impaired, although aspects of their sentence construction were intact.

Functional brain imaging techniques indicate that, for some aspects of visual processing, language background plays a part but not hearing status. For deaf and hearing people who use signing as their first language, structures in the 'visual' parts of the brain were more involved than they were for hearing non-signers. Some brain activity was particular to deaf people irrespective of their knowledge of sign language (e.g. Neville *et al.*, 1997). The age at which verbal language is acquired and the age of onset of deafness appear to have different roles in any cerebral reorganisation occurring during development (Marcotte and Morere, 1990).

Some issues relating to the education of deaf children

This section looks briefly at issues relating to the deaf child's family, cultural 'Deafness' and support in mainstream schools.

Regarding the family, a Northern Ireland survey indicated that 90 per cent of deaf children are born to non-deaf parents (Phoenix, 1988). Among issues with which a family deal are responding to the initial diagnosis and matters arising at times of transition, for example when the child starts school or is entering adolescence. The family's choice of the language to be used with the deaf child is influenced by whether the parents are deaf or hearing, the degree of hearing loss experienced by the child, and other factors.

Some writers, to signal a view of 'cultural Deafness', use 'Deaf' with a capital 'D'. It has been suggested that 'The use of the term "Deaf" is based on the premise that deaf children whose deafness means that they do not acquire spoken language through oral means are likely to develop to become culturally Deaf young people' (Ridgeway, 1998, p. 12). The term 'culturally Deaf' 'refers to those Deaf people who share similar beliefs, values and norms and who identify with other Deaf people' (p. 12). Some writers appear to make an unjustified assumption that people viewed as 'Deaf' necessarily share similar beliefs and values.

Turning to the matter of support in mainstream schools, this relates to understandings of inclusion. Views on that aspect of inclusion concerning the balance of pupils in mainstream and special schools or units range from those preferring placement in the pupil's neighbourhood school (e.g. Deaf Education through Listening and Talking (DELTA), 1997) to separate education in preparation for later integration into society (e.g. British Deaf Association, 1996). Such is the present plethora of supposed rights in education and elsewhere that both of these positions are expressed in terms of rights but are incompatible. Among considerations involved in providing a pattern of support in mainstream are:

◆ the teaching style used by the mainstream teacher;
◆ the pupil's age;
◆ the physical environment of the school;
◆ the mode of communication in which support is provided.

Different issues and emphases arise according to whether support is provided within an oral/aural approach, a TC approach or in British Sign Language (BSL) (these are explained in later sections). Within an oral/aural approach, issues include ensuring amplification aids are in best working order and used optimally and that in-class support is effective. For example, note-taking may be done by a learning support assistant using a laptop computer connected with one used by the pupil, with the learning support assistant close enough to explain any new vocabulary. Within a TC approach, the teacher or learning support assistant may from time to time provide sign support carefully co-ordinated so as not to clash with teacher explanations. Regarding support in BSL, this may involve interpreting the lesson and/or providing pre-tutoring or post-tutoring.

Provision

Professional standards

The *National Special Educational Needs Specialist Standards* (Teacher Training Agency, 1999) states that the three existing mandatory qualifications for teaching pupils with hearing, visual and multi-sensory impairments will remain in force, for 'the foreseeable future' (p. 3). It also sets out standards concerning the effective teaching of pupils having severe and/or complex needs (p. 1). Structured as core standards, extension standards, standards in relation to key SEN roles and responsibilities, and skills and attributes, they are intended as an auditing aid for head teachers and teachers to identify training and development needs. The 'extension standards' give an indication of the knowledge and understanding and the skills associated with teaching children who have hearing impairment.

Teachers with additional specialist skills should know and understand:

i.   How communication and language development are delayed or altered by the effects of mild to profound hearing loss;
ii. auditory-oral approaches to teaching deaf children;
iii. Total communication approaches and the associated range of sign communication systems, including signed English;
iv. the nature of British Sign Language and its use in bilingual/multilingual settings.

(Teacher Training Agency, 1999, p. 16)

i.   how amplification systems make effective use of residual hearing;
ii. a working knowledge of the physics of sound, acoustic phonetics and speech perception;
iii. the anatomy and physiology of the ear and the implications of relevant surgical interventions.

(p. 25)

Teachers with additional specialist skills should have skills in:

i.   designing and implementing a coherent communication programme tailored to the current level of language development/communication of individual pupils;
ii. assessing the residual hearing of pupils and interpreting audiometric information competently;
iii. assessing the amplification needs of individual pupils;
iv. assessing deaf pupils' language and communicative competence, both spoken and signed;

v. making maximum use of pupils' residual hearing and speech reading, and making appropriate and effective use of specialised equipment in differing acoustic environments;

vi. making maximum use of special or additional visual methods to reinforce spoken language;

vii. monitoring speech and language development in deaf pupils and using the information appropriately to support forward planning.

(pp. 17–18)

i. operating and maintaining appropriate audiological and amplification equipment in a variety of acoustic conditions;

ii. making optimal use of residual hearing and speech reading.

(p. 26)

Communication

Communication policies

A survey of communication policies involved contacting schools and units in the United Kingdom providing education for children who are deaf or have hearing impairment (Baker and Knight, 1998, pp. 81–5). These were listed in the *National Deaf Children's Society Directory* (National Deaf Children's Society, 1996). The schools and units were asked to specify their communication policy. Of 31 schools, 15 (48 per cent) specified TC, 7 (23 per cent) oral only, 4 (13 per cent) bilingual, and 5 (16 per cent) declined to specify. Of 468 units, 129 (28 per cent) specified oral only, 104 (22 per cent) TC, 15 (3 per cent) bilingual, and 220 (48 per cent) declined to specify.

An oral/aural approach

An oral/aural approach (hereafter an 'oral' approach) aims to teach children who are deaf or have hearing impairment, and whose parents are hearing, to learn to speak intelligibly and to understand spoken language. The intention is that, later, the person can choose whether to learn sign language such as BSL. Cochlear implants may be made at an early age to promote the use of early use residual hearing. Increasingly earlier identification of deafness is regarded by oralists as enhancing the opportunity to use an oral approach early, although (for example, for very young children) natural gesture is accepted as being important to communication.

Although there have been variations within the approach, some common features are apparent (see the work of the group, DELTA). Some of these features are:

◆ residual hearing is used and enhanced (for example, by hearing aids);
◆ children who are unable to comprehend speech using hearing alone can gain information from lip reading and natural gesture (although, as far as possible, speaking and listening has precedence);
◆ cochlear implants may be used;

◆ there is an emphasis on communicating and the rules of language are assumed to be learnt over time through using language;
◆ every effort is made to provide favourable listening conditions;
◆ active listening skills are encouraged;
◆ the child is encouraged to use contextual clues and knowledge of the world actively to aid communication and understanding.

Total communication

An attempt to clarify what was meant by the term 'total communication' was made in a survey of communication policies mentioned earlier (Baker and Knight, 1998). The 15 schools and 104 units in the United Kingdom specifying a TC policy were asked to select from three definitions of TC:

◆ TC as including the full spectrum of language modes, child devised gestures, the language of signs, speech, speech reading, finger spelling, reading and writing (Denton, 1976, p. 4);
◆ a simple definition indicating speaking and signing at the same time;
◆ a statement of communication policy from Leeds LEA Deaf and Hearing Impaired Support Services (DAHISS) (Leeds Local Education Authority, 1995), which refers to a 'philosophy', bases the choice of methods on children's individual needs, and identifies specific language use.

Of schools, 13 (of 15) (87 per cent) responded and, of units, 72 (of 104) (69 per cent) responded. Regarding schools, 10 preferred the Leeds LEA definition, 1 preferred the Denton definition and 1 preferred an alternative definition. Of units, 16 preferred Denton's definition, 55 the Leeds LEA one, and a single school preferred an alternative definition. No schools or units expressed a preference for the simple definition.

The schools and units were also asked to quantify the extent of their use of four different communication options:

◆ spoken English without sign;
◆ British Sign Language;
◆ sign-supported English;
◆ signed English (SE).

BSL is accepted as a language having its own vocabulary, syntax and grammar but no written form. In BSL, the subject is stated first and then the verbs, adverbs and adjectives. Most signs do not come directly from English words and cannot always be translated in a one-to-one fashion, although finger spelling is used for technical terms and proper names. Signs have meaning not just because of the manual shapes but also from the position of the hands in space, for example in relation to the body of the person who is signing.

Sign-supported English uses signs derived from BSL to support the use of natural English. Users may hold the view that to sign every aspect of spoken English could provide too much information for the child receiving the communication.

SE is a representation, with signs (mainly derived from BSL), of all aspects of spoken English. The vocabulary, plurals, tenses, gender and other features of natural English are all represented. An attempt is made to sign every aspect of what is spoken, thereby facilitating good English.

Responses indicated that schools for deaf children are less likely to be using spoken English without sign regularly and more likely to be using BSL without voice regularly. By contrast, units are more likely to be using spoken English without sign regularly and less likely to be using BSL without voice regularly. Sign-supported English was a dominant choice and was used regularly in both schools and units.

Sign bilingualism

The expression 'sign bilingualism' began to be used in the late 1990s. Sign bilingualism uses both the sign language of the deaf community and the spoken and written language of the hearing community. The goals of sign bilingualism have been described as 'to enable deaf children to become bilingual and bi-cultural, and participate fully in both the hearing society and the "Deaf World"' (Pickersgill, 1998, p. 89).

It has been suggested that some services and schools that see themselves as 'working within a total communication philosophy' may, within that philosophy, 'be adopting a sign bilingual approach for some of these pupils' (Knight and Swanwick, 2002, p. 2). A sign bilingual approach involves the planned, systematic use of both BSL and English, the balance varying according to individual needs (Gregory and Pickersgill, 1997). It has been stated that:

> The outcome of sign bilingual education should be that each child attains levels of competence and proficiency in BSL and English sufficient for their needs as a child and as an adult. The process through which this is achieved should be the planned use of BSL and English before and throughout schooling.
> (Pickersgill and Gregory, 1998, p. 3)

Literacy

Literacy within an oral approach

The difficulties of deaf children with literacy are indicated by often-reported findings that literacy level falls below that typically achieved by hearing peers. Encouraging levels of attainment have been reported in reading using an oral/aural approach with a quarter of the sample reading at or above chronological age on reaching school leaving age (Lewis, 1996). Just as an oral approach to communication highlights meaningful exchanges, so teaching and learning literacy within this approach emphasises creating and exchanging meaning, not decoding words in isolation.

The approach to literacy is interactive in that it accepts that the reader's previous experience, the context of the reading and the text all interact to create meaning. It draws on both top-down and bottom-up approaches as necessary. It has been suggested that three conditions need to be satisfied if reading is to progress well:

- A basic level of linguistic understanding must be established before formal reading programmes are introduced.
- The integrity of reading as a receptive process and as a reflective activity should be preserved.
- The language of ideas that are used to promote deaf children's earliest reading insights must be accessible to them.

(Lewis, 1998, p. 104, paraphrased)

Early reading material should be chosen to ensure that the vocabulary relates to the child's linguistic competence and that meanings relate to the child's experience. Homemade books or the child's version of a story or an event may be used. Helping the pupil with strategies for reading comprehension may be a more effective focus than overemphasising decoding skills, vocabulary and grammar (Banks *et al.*, 1990).

In phonic work, it is essential that sounds that are part of the deaf child's phonic system are used, otherwise phoneme–grapheme correspondence cannot be effectively taught. In later reading, discussing what is read is beneficial. Pre-teaching can help the pupil be prepared for ideas that will come up in the text, allowing fuller participation. Directed Activities Related to Text (DARTs) helps pupils' ability to access text through, for example, paired or small group work and discussion. DARTs is an activity-based approach that enables a pupil to read for meaning despite limited reading skills. Information is gained from the text through structured analysis and reconstruction tasks, which encourage the pupil to regard reading, not as an end in itself, but as a way of learning across the curriculum. (For a recent lucid description of using DARTs with non-deaf pupils see Blum, 2004, Chapter 6.)

In earlier writing, the pupil's communication attempts for a range of purposes will be praised and encouraged by the teacher. Early attempts at writing should be considered in their developmental context (that is, in terms of what is developmentally appropriate) and in the context of the pupil's present linguistic functioning (Lewis, 1998, p. 109). Shared writing activities for various purposes include messages and shopping lists, jokes, postcards, a birthday card, letters and so on. From early stages pupils are encouraged to read back what they have written and as appropriate to self-correct their work.

Story retell programmes (e.g. Lewis, 1998, pp. 107–9) contribute to children remembering what they have read and to self-confidence in writing. The pupil is told a story or reads a story at his present level of verbal recall and understanding. The teacher then asks the pupil to retell the story (unprompted). This is video recorded (as are several subsequent attempts). Each time, the teacher transcribes the videotape verbatim with the pupil. This might be repeated twice a week for two or three weeks, over which time a steady improvement in the pupil's verbal retelling of what he has written is expected to be seen.

Literacy within a sign bilingual approach

In a sign bilingual approach, it is recognised that BSL is the preferred or main language of some children who are deaf. Where this is so, it is maintained that BSL should be used for teaching and learning, including the teaching and learning of spoken and written English. It distinguishes sign language such as BSL and sign systems such as sign-supported English, whose purpose is to encode and to be used in parallel with spoken English. The approach does not accept that sign systems supporting English (simultaneous communication or simcom) necessarily improve a child's English (e.g. Maxwell, 1992).

Because sign language has no orthography, bilingual deaf children have not had the opportunity to gain literacy skills in their primary language. It is important that a pupil's sign language skills are used in literacy teaching (by deaf and hearing adults) for 'presentation, discussion, analysis and explanation of tasks in a way that can bring reading and writing alive for deaf children' (Swanwick, 1998, p. 113). Also important is meta-linguistic understanding developed in sign language and used in constructing the second language (e.g. English). Meta-linguistic awareness involves being able to think and talk about language, its characteristics and structure.

One model of sign bilingual education is that described by Gregory and Pickersgill (1997) in which the prerequisites identified for teaching literacy have principles in common with Scandinavian approaches. These are that:

- BSL is the language of instruction in teaching English.
- BSL and spoken and written English are taught as subjects of the school curriculum.
- BSL skills are considered an essential base on which to successfully build learning English literacy.
- Meta-linguistic skills developed in BSL are expected to be transferable to a pupil's English literacy learning.
- Manually Coded English (MCE) is used for specific teaching purposes such as supporting a pupil's exposure to spoken English.

Various activities support a sign bilingual approach. DARTs are used, offering as they do strategies to approach a text (Swanwick, 1993). Dialogue journals (Baker, 1990) are employed and involve a pupil and an adult communicating with each other by writing in a shared journal. While the adult, in responding, does not correct the pupil's written English, the adults' entries model the correct written English so that the pupil is exposed to this and can learn from it.

Video analysis has been used to make a video bilingual version of a reading scheme, offering opportunities to raise meta-linguistic awareness and improve skills through being able to compare and contrast the two languages (Partridge, 1996). A curriculum published by Leeds Deaf and Hearing Impairment Support Services (DAHISS, 1996) adapts a modern foreign language curriculum for sign bilingual deaf pupils that is used to plan and target English learning objectives and record progress.

It is considered important that deaf and hearing adults who teach literacy in a sign bilingual approach understand the structure of both languages so that they can make explicit comparisons between the languages and anticipate potential areas of difficulty. It has been suggested that:

Alongside . . . support through discussion in sign language, deaf pupils also need plentiful exposure to the different conventions of writing English through wide and guided reading activities. This implies a reading programme which aims to focus the learner's attention on the structures and conventions of written English, in addition to developing their individual reading skills. Deaf children's early writing might then be further supported by the use of structured materials such as writing frames and models.

(Swanwick, 2003, p. 135)

Mathematics

Among approaches to improving the progress of deaf pupils in mathematics are the following.

It is important to focus sufficiently on the language of mathematics. This should help ensure that pupils understand words that may present difficulties, such as 'if' and 'because', and have a good grasp of the specific vocabulary of mathematics, such as 'tangent' and 'decimal'. It should ensure that there is no confusion between words that are used mathematically and words that have one or several everyday meanings, such as 'base' and 'factor'.

The teacher should introduce problems taking into account the order of written language and the order of the required mathematical operation. A study of mathematical problem-solving ability involved 8- to 12-year-old profoundly deaf children of average or above average intelligence. It appeared that problems are easier if the presentation of segments of the problem reflects the order in which the mathematical calculation is carried out (Pau, 1995). This suggests that confidence can be built using problems such as 'Jane is 10 years old. Tom is three years older than Jane. How old is Tom?' before going on to problems in the form of 'Jane is 10 years old. Tom is 13 years old. How much older is Tom than Jane?' once the language has been explained and understood.

It is important to place sufficient emphasis on teaching young children with hearing impairment to count in school, taking care to avoid confusions that might arise between counting and signing. It has been suggested that knowledge of the sequence of counting is a significant predictor of performance on some numerical problems (Nunes and Moreno, 1997a). More emphasis on teaching young children with hearing impairment in school to count is therefore expected to improve their numerical knowledge. It is suggested that the two processes of counting by pointing to objects one at a time and signing be separated to avoid confusion (Nunes and Moreno, 1997b).

The teacher should use the strengths in spatial understanding of children with hearing impairment. A review of 208 studies involving 171,517 deaf participants found that the mean intelligence quotient (IQ) from all the studies was 97 (324 reports); the mean verbal IQ was 86 (32 studies); and the mean non-verbal IQ was 100 (195 studies). For deaf people with deaf parents, it was found that non-verbal IQ was 108, significantly higher than that of hearing people (Braden, 1994). To the extent that it is evident in pupils, this spatial ability can be used as a strength in teaching and learning mathematics.

Information and communications technology

The British Educational Communications and Technology Agency (BECTA) provides useful advice concerning ICT and pupils with SEN including pupils who are deaf (www.becta.org.uk). This includes that any ICT 'solution' must match the needs of the individual pupil, taking into account any additional difficulties he may have. An interactive whiteboard, used with a computer and a projector, is considered a good demonstration tool because it allows the pupil to see what is happening without having to listen to instructions and interpret them. One note of caution is that the light of the whiteboard may take attention away from the speaker, making lip-reading harder. Digital cameras for recording events, visits and pupils' work, and their use with Microsoft PowerPoint software can be motivating for pupils.

Accreditation

Special arrangements that may be made for examinations and course work include:

◆ extra time;
◆ alternative accommodation (for example to ensure optimum acoustics);
◆ means of access to questions (signing, flashcards);
◆ support with coursework.

Children who are deaf and have other disabilities

Definitions of deafness and other disabilities tend to be generic and therefore may not convey important factors such as the interrelationships that may exist between different disabilities. From a study of aetiology and referral patterns of children with hearing impairment in the Trent Health Authority in the United Kingdom, a classification was made of children having 'clinical or developmental disability in addition to hearing impairment' (Fortnum et al., 1996). The classification was further divided into the following areas: cognitive deficit; visual problems; neuro-motor problems; cerebral dysfunction; cranio-facial abnormality; other systemic disorder, including conditions such as asthma, hepatic dysfunction and eczema; and named syndrome.

It was estimated that 39 per cent of children with permanent deafness also had other educationally relevant disabilities (Fortnum et al., 1996). It has also been reported that 35 per cent of children who are severely and profoundly deaf have a visual impairment (Armitage et al., 1995).

Provision for pupils who are deaf and have other disabilities involves taking into account the different difficulties and the way they might interact. For example, if a pupil is identified as having behavioural, emotional and social difficulties, these may be compounded by hearing impairment if information or instructions are misunderstood. This would be further compounded if the hearing impairment were insufficiently recognised.

For communication to be effective for a pupil with hearing impairment and other disabilities or difficulties, a consideration of the child's developmental level and an assessment of his communication skills will be important (McCracken, 1998b, pp. 34–5). A video can be used to help with observations of the 'fine detail of pre-verbal behaviour' to be recorded and assessed (p. 35) relative to the pupil's behaviour and the communicative behaviour of the other communicator. A suitable system of communication will depend on factors such as the pupil's cognitive ability, vision and motor skills and may involve, as well as oral and sign language, alternative and augmentative communication systems.

THINKING POINTS

Readers may wish to consider with reference to a particular school or LEA:

- whether there is a range of venues where pupils with hearing impairment are educated, including mainstream classroom, unit or special resource centre and special school;
- how communication between those working with pupils with hearing impairment is facilitated;
- how interventions are developed, evaluated and refined to ensure an evolving pedagogy.

KEY TEXTS

Gallaway, C. and Young, A. (2003) (eds) *Deafness and Education in the UK – Research Perspectives*, London, Whurr Publishers.

Among the chapters that may be of particular interest to teachers in this volume are: Chapter 6, 'Developing a picture of attainments and progress of deaf pupils in primary schools'; Chapter 7, 'Sign bilingual deaf children's writing strategies: responses to different sources for writing'; and Chapter 8, 'Promoting social and emotional development in deaf children: linking theory and practice'.

Gregory, S., Knight, P. and McCracken, W. *et al.* (eds) (1998) *Issues in Deaf Education*, London, David Fulton Publishers.

In this wide-ranging book, section one, 'The developing deaf child and young person', includes chapters on social development and family life; cognition and deafness; and the education of Asian deaf children. Section two, 'Language and communication', has chapters including oralism; TC; and bilingualism. Section three, 'Teaching and learning', covers such areas as the teaching and learning of literacy; mathematics; ICT; achieving access to a broad and balanced curriculum; and supporting deaf pupils in mainstream settings. 'Audiology' is the subject of section four, while section five deals with 'The context of the education of deaf children' and includes a chapter on the educational attainments of deaf children.

Chapter 4

Provision for deafblind children

INTRODUCTION

This chapter aims to provide the non-specialist teacher with basic information about educating deafblind children. For those wishing to develop their knowledge and skills in this area, such activities as further reading and well-planned visits to schools that educate deafblind children should help the teacher begin to form a foundation from which it should be possible to build the understanding and skills necessary to work with and support a specialist teacher of deafblind children. In this chapter, I define deafblindness, consider its prevalence and incidence, outline some of its causes, and examine implications for a child who is deafblind of whether hearing impairment and/or visual impairment are congenital/early onset or are acquired. The chapter considers the identification and assessment of deafblindness. It explains various approaches to the education of children who are deafblind, focusing mainly on encouraging and developing communication but also touching on mobility and on the child finding out information.

Definitions

An awareness of the implications of different definitions is important when considering deafblindness, because, for example, the range of definitions is associated with a range of possible interventions that may work for pupils who happen to fall into one definition but may not work for pupils covered under another definition. In England and Wales, deafblindness is also referred to as 'multi-sensory impairment'. Sometimes 'deafblind' is written as a single word, which may be taken to suggest the combined effect of being deaf and blind is greater that the sum of its parts. It is also sometimes written as two separate words, 'deaf blind', or as hyphenated words, 'deaf-blind'.

A document by the QCA (1999) states:

> Pupils who are deafblind have both visual and hearing impairments that are not fully corrected by spectacles or hearing aids. They may not be completely

deaf and blind. But the combination of these two disabilities on a pupil's ability to learn is greater than the sum of its parts.

(p. 7)

A child who is deafblind may or may not have other difficulties or disabilities such as profound, severe or moderate learning difficulties, or physical or motor disabilities. Some functional definitions emphasise the effects of deafblindness on communication, mobility and gaining information (e.g. Deaf-Blind Services Liaison Group, 1988). One reason for this emphasis on functional assessment is that assessment of vision and hearing impairment generally does not lead to suggestions for interventions, which functional assessment is designed to do.

In a research project (Porter *et al.*, 1997) on curriculum access for deafblind pupils involving 57 teachers and 82 pupils the objectives were to:

◆ Gather information on the range of strategies (teaching approaches, utilisation of the environment, management of learning, resources, organisation) employed by teachers providing specifically for pupils who are considered deafblind.
◆ Identify how teachers make decisions about the type of strategy to use with a particular pupil or group of pupils, with reference to modifications and adaptations, including the involvement of parents and pupils in the process.
◆ Examine the effectiveness of the range of different strategies used with difference [*sic*] pupil groups, on the basis of criteria identified by teachers in their decision making.

(p. 1)

The project team used various definitions that were in turn based on a definition provided by the New England Center for Deafblind Services as follows:

1   Individuals who are both peripherally deaf or severely hearing impaired and peripherally blind or severely visually impaired according to definitions of 'legal' blindness and deafness; acuity to be measured or estimated in conjunction with a recognition of level of cognitive development supported by medical description of pathology.
2   Individuals who have sensory impairments of both vision and hearing, one of which is severe and the other moderate to severe.
3   Individuals who have sensory impairments of both vision and hearing, one of which is severe, and/or language disabilities, which result in need for special services.
4   Individuals who have sensory impairments of both vision and hearing of a relatively mild to moderate degree and additional learning and/or language disabilities, which result in need for special services or who have been diagnosed as having impairments which are progressive in nature.
5   Individuals who are severely multiply handicapped due to generalized central nervous system dysfunction, who also exhibit measurable impairments of both vision and hearing.

(appendix 1)

One of the findings of the study was that many techniques used with the range of pupils (indicated by the above list 1 to 5) applied to children in schools for pupils with SLD, which often did not take sufficient account of deaf-blindness.

Prevalence and incidence

Murdoch (1997) uses the term 'multi-sensory impairment' and to 'cover the continuum of individuals with congenital or early onset hearing *and* visual impairment' (p. 358, italics in original). In this context, she states that 'multi-sensory impairment' has a very low incidence with estimates suggesting around 0.8 per 10,000 in the UK, which accords with other European countries and the United States of America (p. 356). A document published by the QCA (1999) suggests, 'Recent estimates indicate that the incidence in the UK is about 1.8 per 10,000 of the total population' (p. 7). It is estimated that the incidence of deafblindness among children is around 3 in every 10,000 (Sense, 2004, p. 7).

Regarding school pupils who are described as having 'multi-sensory impairment', in January 2004 in England (DfES, 2004, table 9), there were 350 at School Action Plus representing 0.1 per cent of pupils at this part of the SEN framework and a further 510 pupils with statements of SEN or 0.2 per cent of pupils with statements. The specific figures for ordinary primary and secondary schools and for special schools are as follows. In primary schools, 280 pupils with multi-sensory impairment were at School Action Plus (0.1 per cent of all pupils at School Action Plus in primary schools) and 230 had statements of SEN (0.3 per cent of all pupils with statements in primary schools). In secondary schools, the number was 70 pupils at School Action Plus (0.1 per cent) and 110 with statements of SEN (0.1 per cent). In special schools, where it is much less usual for pupils *not* to have statements of SEN, there were fewer than 5 pupils at School Action Plus (0.2 per cent) and 170 with statements of SEN (0.2 per cent). The figures for special schools included pupils attending maintained and non-maintained special schools but excluded pupils in independent special schools and pupils in maintained hospital schools.

Causes of deafblindness

Infections, genetic or chromosomal syndromes, or birth trauma may cause congenital or early onset deafblindness. Children who are deafblind as a result of such causes often have other impairments such as learning difficulties or physical disabilities.

A parasite, bacteria or virus may transmit infection. Before the rubella vaccination came into widespread use in 1971, the rubella virus was the main cause of deafblindness. (The main factors associated with deafblindness in the early part of the new millennium are premature birth or birth trauma.) Cytomegalovirus (CMV) is a herpes virus that can cause damage to the nervous system of the foetus and can also lead to deafblindness.

Among genetic or chromosomal syndromes that can result in deafblindness is CHARGE syndrome. Thought to have a genetic cause, it is a rare condition the name of which is formed of initials of its common features. These are: *C*oloboma (eye defects); *H*eart defects; choanal *A*tresia (nasal blockage); *R*etardation of growth and developmental delay; *G*enital abnormalities; and *E*ar abnormalities, including deafness. Similarly, Goldenhaar syndrome, which appears to have a genetic cause, can lead to malformations of the ears and to eye abnormalities.

Problems at birth or soon after and associated with deafblindness relate to prematurity, low birth weight, anoxia (insufficient oxygen) or other trauma, or injury.

Acquired deafblindness in children may be the result of genetic syndromes whose effects may emerge later in a child's development, and of accidents or other trauma. Usher syndrome results from a gene defect, which is present from birth but whose effects appear as the child develops. Hearing impairment is present from birth or soon after. Retinitis pigmentosa develops in late childhood or even in adulthood, causing difficulties in changing light conditions and a gradual reduction in peripheral vision. An accident may involve damage to part of the brain involved in processing vision and hearing.

Implications of congenital and acquired hearing and visual impairment

A child who is deafblind has interrelated difficulties in finding out information, communicating with others, and in moving around the environment (Aitken *et al.*, 2000, pp. 3–4). It has been suggested that common patterns are discernible depending on whether either hearing impairment or visual impairment or both are congenital or have a later onset.

When a child experiences congenital or early onset hearing and visual impairment, it is important to acquire and develop communication, perhaps using special signing, and to develop mobility skills and access information.

For a child with congenital or early onset hearing impairment and acquired visual impairment, sight may become progressively more impaired, often in adolescence. Where the hearing impairment was profound, sign language may have been learned, which may need to be adapted because of impaired vision; specialised interpreter services may also be necessary. Access to information may be aided by ICT and mobility training will be helpful.

Where a child has congenital or early onset visual impairment and acquired hearing impairment, the child's early education may have involved learning Braille, mobility and other skills. Reading and writing in Braille may be developed (because speech and hearing were intact earlier) and can assist later learning of deafblind finger spelling, keyboard skills and mobility, and can allow for the later development of Braille skills.

If hearing and visual impairment are both acquired, the child or young person's already developed skills in communication, mobility and accessing information will be affected. The emotional difficulties of losing sight or vision in later childhood or adolescence will require support for both the deafblind young person and his family. Services are provided by Sense, the RNIB and the RNID.

Identification and assessment

Maternity hospital staff, health visitors, parents or others may identify congenital deafblindness. Teachers, parents, specialist teachers, audiologists, ophthalmologists and others may observe later acquired deafblindness. Among the difficulties with identification are matters relating to the definition of deafblindness. It may be argued that a degree of visual impairment that would on its own indicate blindness and a degree of hearing impairment that alone would constitute deafness could, taken together, indicate deafblindness. However, it will be remembered that the combined effect of being both deaf and blind may be considered greater that the sum of its parts. From this perspective, it may be maintained that lower levels of hearing impairment and visual impairment together constitute deafblindness.

Quality Standards in Education Support Services (Sense, 2002) includes standards relating to assessment, emphasising that it should always be concerned with the child as a whole, taking account of the views of the family, the child and professionals (p. 8).

Specialists assess the degree of deafblindness: an audiologist (an audiological scientist trained to perform hearing assessments and fit and monitor hearing aids) and an ophthalmologist (a medical doctor specialising in the diagnosis and treatment of diseases of the eye). Any residual vision or hearing is important and its use should be encouraged. Also contributing to the assessment are the pupil, parent, speech and language therapist, physiotherapist, occupational therapist, educational psychologist and others. The person assessing should be familiar to the child.

It is essential that, when a child is assessed as being deafblind, any other difficulties and disabilities are identified and assessed. But it is equally vital that additional difficulties and disabilities are not wrongly attributed. Because a child who is deafblind learns slowly and requires intensive support, it can be incorrectly assumed that he has cognitive difficulties too. Similarly, motor impairment can be wrongly attributed because the child's movements may be hesitant.

A functional assessment is likely to provide much useful information because it is contextual. As Aitken (1995) points out, 'Instead of abstracting tasks from settings, functional assessment tries to structure the environment to offer opportunities for observing skills in practical use' (p. 9).

In addition to ophthalmological and audiological assessments, the senses of touch, taste, smell and proprioception will be assessed. Assessment of tactile development might include determining if the child can explore objects so as to make fine distinctions between them. Assessing cognitive abilities may include seeking information relating to the child's awareness, attention, memory, curiosity (including problem-solving skills), recognition, imitation, classification, symbolic understanding and number concepts. Communication will be assessed and may be considered in terms of functional and linguistic communication (Eyre, 2000, p. 133).

Functional communication includes assessing, for example, whether the child shows interest in, or participates in, any form of two-way interaction and 'whether the child **associates** any gestures, signs, pictures, objects or words with an activity or person' (Eyre, 2000, pp. 133–4, bold in original). Linguistic communication involves examining the forms of communication used, the functions that language fulfils for the child, and the level of language the child uses, and includes, for example, assessing whether and how the child can 'express wants and needs' and can 'refer back to previous events' (p. 134).

Physical skills may be assessed by a physiotherapist, whose report may include information on 'the child's potential for movement, about dangers to the child associated to certain movements and about medical factors relating to the management of their physical impairments' (Eyre, 2000, p. 135). Such information is used to seek to optimise the child's ability for movement and to ensure the best access to learning. An assessment of social skills might include examining the extent of the child's awareness of himself and others and the child's degree of independence or dependence on other people. Personal factors might include such information as the child's likes and dislikes, what motivates him and how well developed are the child's self-help skills. A report on the child's medical history may include information such as whether the child has been in hospital for long periods. There may be reports from any previous school the child has attended.

Observation relating to assessment involves forming a clear description of what a child did and an interpretation of its context and meaning. The teacher, parents or others may make observations. The purpose of the observation should be clear (for example, to establish what skills the child learns most easily). (For a discussion of approaches to observation and methods of recording observations, see Aitken, 2000, pp. 12–19.)

Among commercial assessments are:

◆ The *Pre-verbal Communication Schedule* (Kiernan and Reid, 1987), used by speech and language therapists and teachers, assesses the communication skill of those who cannot speak or who use a few words, signs or symbols. It is intended for children aged 3 to adults aged 20 and is administered individually, usually taking about 35 to 60 minutes. It is, however, intended to be particularly suited to learners with good visual and hearing skills so its interpretation with deafblind children requires care.

◆ The *Callier Azusa Scale* (Stillman, 1978) is a developmental guide designed for use with deafblind learners.

Also important are assessments relating the child's learning to the curriculum, which might include a judgement about National Curriculum levels and performance descriptor levels (P scales).

Provision

Where a deafblind pupil has some vision, certain strategies and resources mentioned in Chapter 2 can be considered, such as the use of low vision aids and suitable lighting. If the deafblind pupil has some hearing then some of the suggestions made in Chapter 3 can be considered, such as making every effort to provide a suitable listening environment. The remainder of this chapter is concerned with provision and discusses professional standards; the curriculum; communication; mobility; and the child finding out information. The chapter concludes with an outline of a model of intervention.

Professional standards and multi-professional working

The *National Special Educational Needs Specialist Standards*, while stating that the three existing mandatory qualifications for teaching pupils with hearing, visual and multi-sensory impairments remain in force, for 'the foreseeable future',

(Teacher Training Agency, 1999, p. 3), sets out standards concerning the effective teaching of pupils having severe and/or complex needs (p. 1). These are intended as an auditing aid to help head teachers and teachers identify training and development needs. They are structured as core standards, extension standards, standards in relation to key SEN roles and responsibilities, and skills and attributes. The 'extension standards' give an indication of the knowledge and understanding and the skills associated with teaching children who are deafblind.

Teachers with additional specialist skills should know and understand:

i.   the potential impact of the combined effects of sensory loss on learning;
ii. the range and forms/modes of communication used by pupils who are deafblind;
iii. the roles of the different senses in combining to produce environmental awareness, and the kinds of sensory information potentially available to a pupil with auditory and visual impairments;
iv. the use of objects of reference.

(p. 16)

i.   How social isolation and emotional deprivation created by deafblindness may contribute to challenging behaviour.

(p. 22)

i.   the basic principles of orientation and mobility for pupils who are deafblind.

(p. 25)

Teachers with additional specialist skills should have skills in:

i.   Providing opportunities for pupils to have increased tactile, proprioceptive and kinaesthetic awareness during daily routines and planned activities;
ii. using specific visual, auditory and tactile methods to help pupils understand the functional use of objects, to gain information about the environment, and use visual, auditory and tactile cues to initiate and terminate interactions;
iii. assessing functional hearing, vision, communication and general development;
iv. optimising the use of residual vision and/or hearing;
v.   using receptive and expressive communication, employing means and approaches appropriate to the needs of the individual child.

(p. 17)

i.   Maintaining and evaluating the use of appropriate auditory and visual aids.

(p. 26)

In *Quality Standards in Education Support Services* (Sense, 2002) the standards relating to the school years include that pupils should have access to a qualified teacher of children who are described as deafblind or multi-sensory impaired 'throughout their school years' (p. 13 standards SY1). Also, there should be evidence that 'There are regular visits from the deafblind/MSI teacher to ensure the child's full access to learning opportunities' (p. 13 standards SY2).

Other professionals who may have been involved with the deafblind child and the child's parents include: the health visitor; general practitioner; ear, nose and throat specialist; ophthalmologist; orthoptist (a technician who provides exercises aimed at restoring or developing the co-ordination of the eye system); a technician dealing with hearing aids; audiologist; speech and language therapist; physiotherapist; occupational therapist; social worker; and educational psychologist. When it is remembered that several of the particular personnel may have changed over the years, the number of people with whom the parent and child come into contact is daunting. This emphasises the importance of the teacher and the school drawing together information and advice from many sources and using them to make educational judgements about what will enable the child to learn best.

The curriculum and cross-curricular skills

In general the curriculum for pupils who are deafblind will in its content and structure have regard to the National Curriculum (including support such as the use of signing or Moon); use the flexibilities of the National Curriculum (such as working at a lower level than most children of the same age); and may draw on child developmental models, especially models of early communication. It will take full account of the importance of the environment, the communication partner and other 'systems' influences. It is considered important that there are opportunities for free play and self-occupation between adult-led tasks and that the timetable includes activities that the pupil appears to enjoy or at least in which he is willing to participate (Pease, 2000, p. 48). For discussion of curriculum and teaching and learning aspects of personal, social and health education (PSHE) see Clark (2000, pp. 83–118), who discusses everyday activities (eating and drinking and dressing); sex education; challenging behaviour; physical changes; emotional changes; human reproduction; personal hygiene; residential education; mobility; and religious education.

Cross-curricular skills and understanding may be audited and recorded using a skills matrix (e.g. Hodges, 2000, p. 177), which is a way of presenting a plan set out in columns and rows of how key targets are integrated across curriculum areas. For example, the left-hand column might list regular or daily activities such as 'morning greeting' and 'drink'. A key target such as 'choosing between two activities' might head the other columns, with elements listed below to show how the target is applied in different situations. In 'morning greeting' the choice might be between greeting by a 'sign' or a 'song', while in the drink session the choice might be between 'apple' or 'biscuit'. As targets and their elements are identified in the columns, the rows indicate how a particular daily activity contributes to the targets.

Communication

General requirements

Communication requires 'someone to communicate with (a giver and receiver); something about which to communicate; a reason or intention to communicate; and some means of communicating' (Aitken, 2000, p. 24 and see also pp. 24–9).

Factors impeding communication for deafblind pupils include: 'direct effects of sensory impairment; effects of motor impairment; effects of ill health and medication; lack of opportunities to interact; lack of interactive strategies; lack of information; lack of knowledge about the world; poor self-image; impaired communication from other people; and "doing for" the child' (p. 40).

The teacher will need to be aware of the ways in which communication and interaction typically develops in children. This underpinning of knowledge of typical development will inform the setting of suitable goals for learning of pupils who are deafblind. Also, the teacher and school will provide opportunities to interact naturally in the context of activities that have meaning for the pupil. At the same time, the teacher will take account of the specific ways in which a child who is deafblind develops. For example, the teacher will need to identify and build upon tiny responses and idiosyncratic behaviours. Object cues might be used to signal activities. Above all the teacher should 'exploit every avenue to help the child develop a sense of agency, the understanding that he can affect his environment and "make things happen"' (Pease, 2000, p. 45).

Some approaches to encourage communication

Among approaches aimed at encouraging and developing communication are: Intensive Interaction, co-creative communication, resonance work, co-active movement and signing, burst-pause activities, routines and 'scripts' and hand-over-hand work, each of which is considered in turn below.

Nind and Hewett (2001, p. 17) have described the aims and outcomes of Intensive Interaction as follows: 'By using Intensive Interaction we are trying to help the person learn fundamentals of communication – eye contacts, facial expressions, turn taking'. Intensive Interaction (Nind and Hewett, 1994) can involve encouraging interaction as it were for its own sake or can enable interaction with other children and help the pupil gain access to the curriculum through improving language and interpersonal behaviour. It involves 'regular, frequent interactions between the practitioner (be it teacher, carer, professional from a range of disciplines) and the individual with learning disabilities, in which there is no task or outcome focus, but in which the primary concern is the quality of the interaction itself' (Hewett and Nind, 1998, p. 2).

Co-creative communication emphasises the importance of the relationship between the child and the communication partner. The relationship has been described as 'symmetrical' (Nafstad and Rodbrøe, 1999) and it has been stated that one of the roles of partners is to recognise the deafblind pupil as an extraordinary version of oneself, leading to a more equal relationship (Nafstad, 2000).

Resonance work (van Dijk, 1989) tends to be an initial form of encouragement of communication that involves an adult reflecting back to the child the child's movements or vocalisations, the idea being that this encourages the child's awareness of self. In other words, the adult resonates the child's actions and vocalisations, continuing when the child continues and stopping when the child stops.

In co-active movement, the child tends to be more aware of the adult and of the idea of interchange than is the case with resonance work. The adult and child are in close bodily contact; for example, the child may be sitting on the adult's knee. The movements (e.g. swaying from side to side a number of times, or bouncing on the adult's knee a number of times) are carried out in a sequence until the child is familiar with them. Once the child has grasped the pattern, the adult can evoke 'signal behaviour' by, for example, interrupting the sequence, observing the pupil's reaction and responding immediately to reinforce the signal (Pease, 2000, p. 76). The closeness of the physical contact is gradually lessened and the pupil may hold the adult's hands for co-active movement.

In a burst-pause activity, the adult ensures that there is time for the pupil to respond and provides prompts for further activity. At first the adult leads the activity then stops, allowing the pupil to pick up the activity. The adult then keeps the activity going until the next pause. For example, if the task is making a cooking mixture, the adult will first lead then stop to allow the child to continue. The adult will then encourage the activity until the next pause.

Where routines are intended to encourage early communication, it is helpful if they are predictable, frequent, and occur at the same time and in the same place, perhaps each day. Such routines might be built into mealtimes or a movement sequence. More generally, routine, so long as it does not become over-rigid, provides security and predictability and helps learning because it involves repetition. It gives a framework in which a child can come to recognise sequences: what happened before, what is happening now and what happens next. As an aid to communication, routine can encourage the pupil to signal as he anticipates the next part of a sequence of events.

'Scripts' are one way of helping ensure that routines are followed closely in the earlier stages of developing them. These involve recording and following an action sequence such as a mealtime routine in steps in which the actions carried out by the adult and the actions of the child are specified. Choice can be built into these steps so that they are not completely rigid. As routines become established, the structure can be varied through changing what is anticipated, providing increasing choice for the pupil.

In working hand-over-hand, the adult moves the child's hands slowly and with sensitivity to show him how to do something. In working in this way, the adult is careful to respond to any signs of discomfort or resistance from the child. If a child's main source of information is the hands, he may not like another person as it were taking them over and may resist. The adult can encourage learning hand-over-hand but should not, of course, force it.

Using non-symbolic communication

Symbolic communication involves something standing for a concept, such as an object, a picture, a manual sign or a spoken word, allowing the child to refer to things other than the here and now. *Non*-symbolic communication is direct and does not rely on symbolic understanding. Examples are reflexive responses, signals, and place or object cues.

Reflexive responses are very basic responses to the external environment, or to the internal bodily environment such as hunger. Examples are stilling, changes in body tone, and cooing or shouting. While the child has no control over these responses, and they have not been taught, they can suggest what a child is aware of and his likes and dislikes.

Signals have been described as 'deliberate responses to the environment made with a specific end in view' (Pease, 2000, p. 59). They may include (depending on the child's mobility) picking up a desired object or pushing an object away, rolling to one side to get away from an activity, or pulling at a person's hand. Such actions may not always be intentionally communicative but, where the teacher and others respond as if they were so, the child may learn that they have a certain effect. The child is encouraged to attract attention before making such a signal. Place or object cues are used in structured routines so that certain objects and places come to typify activities for the child. When this link is made, the child can, for example, use the object to indicate a desire for an activity.

Symbolic communication

This section examines objects of reference; pictures and visual symbols; and manual sign language, speech and aided communication.

Object cues, where certain objects come to typify activities for the child, have already been mentioned as examples of non-symbolic communication. It was stated that, when a link is made between an object and an activity, the child could, for example, use the object to indicate a desire for an activity. Understanding of an object of reference may develop from this. The object of reference may be used to indicate an event or activity when it may not be happening in the present, perhaps to remember something that has happened (a ribbon to remember a present) or something that is to happen later (a piece of swimming costume to indicate that the child will go swimming later that day). Also the object of reference is not the actual object; for example, it is not the real present that was received. It is symbolic of the object or event. So-called calendar boxes (Pease, 2000, pp. 77–9) use sequences of objects of reference to indicate the order of activities and events in the pupil's day, acting as a sort of tangible timetable. Tactile objects of reference may be used to indicate a proposed activity; signal a proposed change of activity; help the pupil anticipate a task; or help the pupil make a choice or decide on an activity.

Pictures can be drawn by the teacher and initially can be related to objects of reference with which the child is familiar. For example, if an object of reference for swimming is a piece of coloured 'float', the picture might be a drawing of this using the same colour. The object of reference and the picture could be presented together for some time until it appeared that the pupil was able to make the link that the picture on its own could represent the activity of swimming. A picture is a further step away from the real activity of swimming than the object of reference, so it may take some time and effort before the link is made. But, once this is achieved, the opportunity to use pictures as symbols of activities, people or events enables the pupil to communicate in a more practicable way. Similarly, photographs can be used, especially if what they represent is clear and the photograph is uncluttered. The use of digital cameras enables photographs of an activity to be taken and shown to a child so that the link between the activity and the photograph when it is shown at another time may be made easier.

Visual symbols are usually agreed systems for communication, although these can be supplemented by symbols more personalised to the pupil. Makaton symbols may be employed where the child also uses Makaton manual signs, although for some pupils the connection between movements with the hands in three-dimensional space and two-dimensional representations may be obscure.

Tactile symbols may be used where a pupil understands objects of reference but has difficulty seeing or interpreting pictures and visual symbols. Developing on from an understanding of tactile objects of reference, some pupils may be able to use tactile symbols such as Moon script to recognise letters or words.

Parts of an object can be used so long as they convey to the pupil what is intended. For example, a length of leather rein can indicate horse riding. Symbols involving texture and shape can be used. For example, different shapes can represent different timetabled subjects or activities. Different textures can indicate various times of the day (morning, afternoon, night). Materials with raised outlines, perhaps using a Thermoform machine, can represent items or events and can act as a link to literacy using the Moon script.

Miniature objects may be used, for example a toy horse used to represent the activity of horse riding. The teacher will need to ensure that the pupil is making the link between the real horses and the activity and the miniature object, perhaps by encouraging the pupil to explore the miniature object while at horse riding and gradually introducing the miniature object to stand for the activity when it is, for example, scheduled later in the day.

Turning to manual sign language, earlier chapters in this volume concerning hearing impairment and deafblindness discussed different manual sign languages: BSL, Makaton, SE and sign-supported English. For a child who is deafblind, using sign language might involve drawing with the finger the shapes of the letters of a word on the other person's hand. Another form of signing involves the communication partner tapping a position on the other person's fingers and palm to correspond to different letters of the alphabet. For signing to be effective for pupils who are deafblind, the school and others need to take account of the pupil's physical, cognitive and visual skills. In finger spelling, words and sentences from speech are spelled out using a particular hand shape for each alphabetic letter. The deafblind manual alphabet is based on the visual alphabet with modifications to enable the sender to spell out words on to the receiver's left hand. Finger spelling can be used in its own right, accompanied or unaccompanied by spoken English. Or it can be used to supplement manual sign language by spelling out names or features for which there may be no sign in the system. In co-active signing, the adult guides the pupil's hands through the shape and movement of the sign.

The school and others will try to encourage potential for developing speech. This may involve the pupil using hearing aids and the school ensuring that the auditory environment is optimal.

Various resources can further aid communication. Computer-aided communication may involve the pupil having a voice production device with a computer-based bank of words and sentences that can be produced by pressing the keyboard keys. A computer's graphic capabilities can be used to produce symbols similar to those used in symbol systems. A communication book is a collection of tactile symbols on pages of a book that the child can turn to in order to convey different messages. The symbols can be accompanied by written messages so that the child can turn to a particular page in the book and show it to others who do not understand the symbol system in order to convey a message. For example, in a shop, such a book can be used to request different items.

Using communication during an activity and group work

An example of using communication during an activity is provided by Pease (2000, p. 52). The setting is a cookery lesson with a pupil aged 16 years who is profoundly deaf and who is thought to be totally blind. The strategies with this particular pupil include preceding the visit to the kitchen by the teacher putting objects of reference on a board and the teacher putting the pupil's hand on her walking frame to signal that it is time to go to the kitchen. The teacher puts the pupil's hand on the door handle to indicate 'here is the kitchen' and places the pupil's hand on the chopping board to signal 'here are the ingredients'. When the teacher taps the pupil's hand on the pupil's chest, it indicates 'you do it, please'. When the teacher puts the pupil's hand on the teacher's chest it indicates 'I'll do this bit'. The pupil's signals include standing up ('I know where I'm going'); sitting and co-operating ('I know what I'm doing'); and shaking her head from side to side ('I'm not happy').

Group work requires careful structuring for a child who can neither see nor hear what other participants are doing and saying. The pupil will need to be taught behaviours such as turn-taking; when it is time to listen and to speak; and similar features of group work that other pupils will tend to pick up with less effort. For such reasons, the child who is deafblind may initially sit close to the teacher or an adult who can prompt the child as necessary and provide cues as to what is expected.

Mobility

Being unable to use hearing when vision is impaired and being unable to use vision when hearing is impaired, a child who is deafblind has difficulties moving around, especially in unfamiliar surroundings. Improving mobility begins with developing trust with a child and building the pupil's confidence and motivation to move. For pupils with additional difficulties, such as physical disabilities, or difficulties with movement and co-ordination, clearly mobility is going to be more difficult and any aspect of the environment that can aid mobility needs to be given consideration.

The provision of a tactile environment (e.g. QCA, 1999) recognises that it is important for a pupil who is deafblind to be able to explore and build a 'mental map' of each space. Features aiding this include 'a strip of carpet across a hall, a handrail between a playground entrance and the play equipment, a textured surface at the top and bottom of a flight of stairs' (p. 28). It is also suggested that a mental map is easier to build up and maintain if furniture is kept in the same position, routes through a room or building are kept free of obstacles, and tactile clues are added to objects such as specific lockers or doors. Flooring may also be laid out in different textures for different purposes (quiet area, play area) and there may be contrasting textures on the walls in a corridor (p. 29). Tactile pictures can also be used as wall clues.

Finding out information and encouraging meaningful experiences

Difficulties in finding out information apply to television, radio, publications, forms, bills, tickets, the facial expressions of others, surrounding and distant objects and so on. Being unable to access such information makes it more difficult to build up knowledge of the world, which in turn affects communication.

Using information in this broad sense as what one perceives and interprets, it will be evident that, for a child who is deafblind, information is reduced or distorted when compared with that received by a child with full vision and hearing. Learning that, to other pupils, would be incidental is limited and it is therefore often necessary to provide such experiences in a more structured and planned way. Also, the teacher will ensure that information is provided to encourage the deafblind pupil to exercise choice, for example by deciding on an item of clothing according to texture. Also important are 'structured opportunities within which to interact with people, the physical environment, objects, places and activities' (Aitken, 2000, p. 23). Part of this is the provision of routines to encourage anticipation and help the pupil begin to make sense of a sequence of events.

It is clearly important that a pupil who is deafblind recognises an activity, works with other people and learns from experience. In order to accomplish this, the pupil has to be able to identify and recognise an object, the activity performed, the time when it is done, or the person with whom it is done. Identifying and recognising a place in which activities often occur is part of this sort of orientation too. To help a pupil identify and recognise an object, the teacher and other adults may all agree to identify the same distinctive features of the object. For example, an adult co-actively lifting a hairbrush with the child and feeling the bristles and then the handle before brushing the hair can help the child to identify the item (Hodges, 2000, p. 195). Gradually, different brushes may be introduced, identifying the same features so that the pupil's notion of what a brush is can be slightly extended. A place such as a room can be identified by encouraging the pupil to move in the room and by indicating features that are distinctive to the room, such as a chopping board in a kitchen or a bed in a bedroom. Identifying others is helped if the person has a feature that is identified and recognised, such as a necklace that they always wear and that is held for the child to touch as an indication of who the person is. Other identifying features include items of clothing such as a bracelet and distinctive features such as plaited hair.

Further familiarity with items, their use and the time when things are done can be combined in such occasions as meal times. The pupil may get knives, forks and spoons from a cutlery drawer, identify each and lay the table for lunch.

A model of intervention

Murdoch (1997) suggests a model of intervention that draws together some of the approaches outlined in the present chapter. It comprises four aspects (context, content, process and purpose). For the aspect of *context* (addressing the questions 'who?', 'when?' and 'where?'), among suggestions for optimising the 'learning situation' are clearly identifying each person who is working with the pupil, for example by a tactile cue and a greeting routine, and signalling activities by sensory cues. Regarding the aspect of *content*, which concerns the question 'what?', optimising the learning situation involves such features as that 'priorities are decided from assessment, especially of the learner's interests'. Turning to the aspect of *process*, addressing the question 'how?', approaches include 'developing attachment between learner and educator', and 'encouraging the learner to control situations rather than to respond passively'. In relation to the aspect of *purpose*, dealing with the question 'why?', optimising the learning situation may involve increasing the pupil's autonomy and sense of self-worth (Murdoch, 1997, p. 364).

THINKING POINT

Readers may wish to consider:

◆ steps that may be taken to develop further understanding of provision for deafblind children, such as school visits to observe lessons and other aspects of provision, discussion with specialist teachers of deafblind children, and further reading.

KEY TEXTS

Aitken, S., Buultjens, M., Clark, C. *et al.* (eds) (2000) *Teaching Children who are Deafblind: Contact, Communication and Learning*, London, David Fulton Publishers.

This book, written by specialists working in the English and Scottish educational systems, introduces approaches to educating deafblind children, with particular chapters on personal and social development, assessment, the curriculum and teaching and learning.

Qualifications and Curriculum Authority (1999) *Shared World – Different Experiences: Designing the Curriculum for Pupils who are Deafblind*, London, QCA.

Intended for SEN advisers in LEAs or special schools, this publication provides guidance on planning, teaching and evaluating a curriculum for deafblind children.

Sense (2004) *Reaching Out: A Toolkit for Deafblind Children's Services*, London, Sense.

This publication indicates the importance of social care services to the well-being of children who are deafblind and their families and to their social needs outside school. It also briefly explains the nature of deafblindness; the impact of deafblindness on communication, independence skills and sensory information; and how local services should identify and assess deafblind children. The booklet explains the range of services that are appropriate and the importance of co-ordination.

Chapter 5

Physical and motor disability, and medical conditions

INTRODUCTION

While the special educational focus of this chapter is physical and motor disability, it includes a consideration of some conditions often referred to as medical conditions. The relationship between medical conditions, physical disability and mobility is implicit in guidance on data collection for types of SEN (DfES, 2003). This points out: 'There are a number of *medical conditions* associated with *physical disability* which can impact on *mobility*. These include cerebral palsy, heart disease, spina bifida and hydrocephalus, and muscular dystrophy. Pupils with physical disabilities may also have sensory impairments, neurological problems or learning difficulties' (p. 7, italics added).

This chapter examines the relationship between medical conditions and SEN, and the prevalence of physical disability. Specifically, I consider spina bifida and hydrocephalus, muscular dystrophy and cerebral palsy, spinal curvatures (which may be the result of medical conditions such as spina bifida, cerebral palsy or muscular dystrophy, but can have other causes) and limb loss or damage. The chapter then examines epilepsy, cystic fibrosis, diabetes and asthma. With regard to each of these conditions, I seek to define the condition, consider its causes and symptoms and set out the educational implications. Finally, I draw together some of the approaches and provision relating to the education of pupils with physical and motor difficulties and medical conditions.

Medical conditions and SEN

As this chapter discusses certain medical conditions, it may be helpful to outline the relationship between medical conditions in general and SEN. A medical diagnosis (or a disability) does not necessarily imply an SEN. This means that many pupils may have a diagnosis of a medical condition but not have a difficulty in learning or a disability that leads to a learning difficulty that requires additional educational provision. In short, they do not have an SEN.

Some pupils, however, while not considered as having an SEN, have medical conditions requiring correct management in order that the pupil's access to education is not hindered. The *Special Educational Needs Code of Practice* recognises the 'significant impact' that medical conditions may have on a child's experiences and the way the pupil functions at school (DfES, 2001a, 7: 65). Where the influence is direct, the condition may 'affect cognitive or physical abilities, behaviour and emotional state' (7: 65). Indirect impact includes that access to education may be disrupted unavoidably because of the necessity for treatment. Also, there may be psychological effects on children and their families of 'serious or chronic illness or disability' (7: 65).

The *Code* states that 'The effects of the medical condition may be intermittent and their impact on the child's function in school can vary at different stages of their school career. This may reflect changes in the school curriculum, changes in the individual child and changes in the peer group, for example with the onset of puberty' (7: 65). The *Code* points out the importance of close collaboration between the school, the child's parents and others such as the child's GP to help ensure that the pupil makes the best progress and is not excluded unnecessarily from any part of the school curriculum (7: 66). The school's system of pastoral care should allow pupils to discuss any problems, including health-related ones, with a suitable person, such as an educational psychologist or a counsellor (7: 67).

Minimum national standards have been set for the education of children unable to attend school because of medical needs. These are to be found in the document, *Access to Education for Children and Young People with Medical Needs* (DfES, 2001c), which applies to pupils who are physically ill or injured as well as pupils with mental health problems. The provision for such children includes the hospital school or hospital teaching service; home teaching; or an integrated home and hospital education service. School policy statements should include information such as strategies for ensuring support in cases of long-term absence, 'including the provision of assessment and curriculum plans within 5 working days and work programmes on a termly basis' (p. 11, section 2.7). The policy should also cover 'issues related to pupils with statements of special educational needs' (p. 11, section 2.7).

Prevalence

Regarding 'physical disability', in January 2004 in England (DfES, 2004, table 9), there were 7,700 pupils at School Action Plus representing 2.2 per cent of pupils at this part of the SEN framework and a further 16,960 pupils with statements of SEN or 7.2 per cent of pupils with statements. The specific figures for ordinary primary and secondary schools and for special schools are as follows. In primary schools, 5,180 of pupils with physical disability were at School Action Plus (2.4 per cent of all pupils at School Action Plus in primary schools) and 6,610 had statements of SEN (9.6 per cent of all pupils with statements in primary schools). In secondary schools, there were far fewer at School Action Plus than in primary, being 2,340 (1.8 per cent), and a smaller number than in primary with statements of SEN, 5,200 (6.6 per cent). In special schools, where it is much less usual for pupils *not* to have statements of SEN, there were only 190 pupils at School Action Plus (11.3 per cent) and 5,140 with statements of SEN (5.8 per cent). The figures for special schools included pupils attending maintained and non-maintained special schools but excluded pupils in independent special schools and pupils in maintained hospital schools.

Spina bifida and hydrocephalus

Spina bifida is a condition in which one or more spinal vertebrae fail to close properly, exposing the nerves. The effects of the condition are influenced by two main factors: the site of the lesion (at which part of the spinal column the vertebrae are separated) and the extent of damage to the nerves. Many children with spina bifida have hydrocephalus, a condition in which the obstructed flow of cerebral spinal fluid leads to the enlargement of brain ventricles. Both genetic and environmental factors appear to be implicated in the occurrence of spina bifida and hydrocephalus. Symptoms associated with spina bifida and hydrocephalus include:

- ◆ total or partial paralysis of the legs;
- ◆ paralysis of the bladder and bowel;
- ◆ difficulties with activities involving the arms and hands;
- ◆ poor fine motor skills;
- ◆ poor balance;
- ◆ problems with circulation;
- ◆ visual impairment.

Children with spina bifida may require mobility aids such as callipers or a wheelchair, and a catheter to assist urination. They will require physiotherapy and perhaps occupational therapy and speech and language therapy. Children with hydrocephalus may be treated by the use of a 'shunt': a fine tube surgically inserted into a cavity of the brain so that it drains away excess fluid to be disposed of elsewhere (usually in the chest cavity or the abdominal cavity). There are health implications that require immediate referral to a GP or a hospital, for example if the shunt is blocked, perhaps giving rise to symptoms including drowsiness, squint and headache.

Within the areas of personal, social and health development, part of the educational implications entails ensuring that facilities are available that enable pupils to be as little constrained by the condition as is practicable. Within the school, children may need access to adapted toilet facilities and help with dressing, and younger pupils may need help changing their catheter.

Similarly, mobility should be aided as necessary. This might include wheelchair access to the school building and to the classroom(s) and sufficient room to manoeuvre comfortably around the classroom as necessary. Other suggestions include seating near the door so that there is easy access to and from the class and flexibility in the time of arrival at and departure from lessons to avoid times when corridors are full of pupils. Other pupils may help by collecting items required for a lesson (Kenward, 1997, p. 32).

Motor difficulties and spatial problems may lead to particular challenges with handwriting and number work, and a learning support assistant may therefore help with practical tasks or act as an amanuensis. Similarly, an amanuensis may be requested as part of special arrangements when examinations are taken. The use of ICT can provide an alternative means of presenting and recording work.

While some pupils with spina bifida attain at the same levels as children who do not have the condition, others, especially if they also have hydrocephalus, may have severe to moderate learning difficulties. Absences from school may also lead to the pupil attaining at a lower level than he otherwise might. The pupil may have speech and language difficulties, including difficulties with the comprehension of language, that may require the help of a speech and language therapist. This may be through direct intervention or through a consultancy role in which learning support assistants or others work within a programme developed and supervised by a speech and language therapist. If a visual impairment makes it difficult for the pupil to judge distance or direction, multi-sensory teaching methods can help by drawing on other senses.

Muscular dystrophy

Muscular dystrophies are types of genetic, progressive muscular disorders in which breakdown of muscle fibre leads to weak and wasted muscles. While some types affect both sexes, Duchenne muscular dystrophy, the most common form, affects boys exclusively. The life expectancy of children and young people with muscular dystrophy is shortened and some die in their late teens.

The main symptom is a gradual weakening of the muscles because they are damaged and not regenerated adequately, so that the muscle is replaced by fibrous tissue and fat. There may be times of remission as well as periods of rapid deterioration. Pupils may require aids to mobility such as callipers and walking aids and, as the condition progresses, will need a manual or powered wheelchair. Some pupils have metal rods surgically implanted in the back to help maintain an upright posture. Children with muscular dystrophy require regular physiotherapy.

In the areas of personal, social and health development, the pupil may need, as the condition progresses, increasing amounts of help with such things as using the toilet, dressing and eating. Later, one-to-one support, perhaps from a learning support assistant, may be necessary throughout the day, both during and outside lesson times. Particular sensitivity is needed from all staff in schools and other professionals as pupils reach adolescence and may be becoming increasingly dependent, as their peers are getting more and more independent. Counselling may be offered (if parents agree) to help the pupil come to terms with his shorter life expectancy. This is provided by local support groups or by the organisation CRUSE (see addresses).

Mobility should be aided as required. Arrangements for this are similar to those for pupils with spina bifida. For example, they might include wheelchair access to the school building and to the classroom(s) and room to move around the classroom as necessary. The pupils may have seating near the door to allow easy access to and from the class and flexibility in the time of arrival at and departure from lessons to avoid busy times in corridors. The pupil may need support in class to help him use equipment and resources (Kenward, 1997, p. 34).

Most children with muscular dystrophy have levels of intelligence typical of other children of the same age. But, as the illness progresses, the pupil may be more frequently absent from school and progress in school subjects may therefore be slower. Generally, especially as the condition progresses, the pupil will become tired easily. This suggests reviewing the pupil's whole curriculum to ensure that the activities and the way the lessons are dispersed throughout the day and the week keep demands realistic. Homework is usually waived. Handwriting may be affected as the condition weakens the arms and hands. For practical activities, the teacher will need to pitch the level of work to that of which the pupil is physically capable. ICT may be used as an alternative way of recording work.

If the pupil has rods surgically inserted in the back he is vulnerable if knocked, so that contact sports cannot be played.

In examinations, a scribe may be used and extra time allowed. In careers guidance particular sensitivity is needed.

Cerebral palsy

Cerebral palsy is a physical impairment affecting movement and has different forms: spasticity, athetosis and ataxia. Spasticity is characterised by disordered control of movement. Athetosis involves some loss of control of posture and a tendency to make involuntary movements. Ataxia is typified by an unsteady gait and problems with balance, and sometimes a child with ataxic cerebral palsy has irregular speech and tremorous hand movements. A child may experience a mixture of the above types with different effects. Cerebral palsy is caused by damage to the developing brain. This can be brought about by asphyxia (before, during or after birth); brain haemorrhage; or illness such as meningitis, encephalitis or jaundice. Symptoms may include:

- quadriplegia (in which all four limbs are affected), hemiplegia (in which one side of the body is affected) or paraplegia (in which either the arms or the legs are affected);
- loss of control of movement and increased reflex activity;
- limited range of movement;
- stiff and/or immobile legs;
- poor control of the head;
- difficulty with articulation;
- epilepsy (affecting about a third of children with cerebral palsy);
- problems with visual perception.

Most children require a structured programme of physiotherapy. Pupils using a wheelchair may need to spend part of the day standing, using specialised equipment. Advice is sought from the local health authority physiotherapy and occupational therapy departments. There are particular medical implications where the child has epilepsy (see later section).

In terms of personal, social and health development, some pupils may need help with many tasks such as dressing, using the toilet and eating, while others will require limited help with only some activities. As with pupils with muscular dystrophy, particular sensitivity is needed as pupils reach adolescence when they may be becoming more dependent while peers are becoming more independent.

Regarding mobility, pupils may require wheelchair access, seating near the classroom door and flexibility of arrival and departure times to lessons. Also, the pupil may need seating at a desk with ankles at right angles resting on the floor or on a foot block. Particular care is required if the pupil is seated on the floor, as posture is important and chairs are more comfortable.

Most children with cerebral palsy come within the average range of intelligence. Help and/or adapted equipment may be needed for practical tasks depending on the degree of the pupil's disability. The use of ICT can aid in recording work and there are other alternative recording strategies such as using a tape recorder for some activities or using an interactive whiteboard (Hull Learning Services, 2004a, p. 18). 'Switches' may be used.

Children with severe forms of the disability may require augmented communication devices such as voice synthesisers. This will require the teacher and learning support assistant to use the system under the guidance of a speech and language therapist. Where the pupil has speech and language difficulties that may not be as severe, this may involve the child working on a speech and language programme developed by the speech and language therapist and delivered by support staff. Special arrangements may be made for examinations, such as an amanuensis and/or extra time.

Spinal curvatures

Three types of spinal curvature are identified: scoliosis, kyphosis and lordosis. In scoliosis, one hip is higher than the other and one shoulder blade is more prominent than the other. With kyphosis, there is a posterior curvature of the spine leading to shortened stature and decreased lung capacity. Lordosis is a forward curvature of the spine when it is viewed from the side. Spinal curvatures are often the result of conditions such as spina bifida, muscular dystrophy or cerebral palsy but may also develop as a result of tumours, infections and metabolic diseases. The symptoms are somewhat self-explanatory given the condition: shortened stature, altered posture and decreased lung capacity.

A body brace or jacket may be used to correct the posture. Corrective surgery may be used to fuse some of the spinal vertebrae and/or insert metal rods in the back to help the child maintain a more upright posture. Where pain-killing medication is prescribed, the school might administer this.

Pupils may experience low self-esteem because of their physical difference and PSHE and good pastoral support can help improve this. If the pupil requires frequent hospital treatment he may miss schoolwork, although there may be teaching in the hospital for pupils who are staying for longer periods. Pupils may experience pain and as a result become very tired, so the curriculum may need to be adapted.

Some pupils may not be able to take part in the usual school physical activities. They may need to be 'disapplied' from physical education or an adapted course of physical education may be planned. Rough physical play may be too risky and a quiet place for break time leisure activities might be helpful. Seating arrangements may need to be adapted to provide for difficulties with posture.

The pupil may require extra time to travel around school, so flexible start and finish times for lessons can help.

Limb loss or damage

Limb deficiency may be partial or total and can be congenital or acquired (for example, through accident, surgery or disease). Pupils may be fitted with artificial limbs (prostheses). Depending on the particular limb deficiency, the pupil may use a wheelchair, crutches or a walking aid.

In PSHE, pupils with limb deficiencies should be encouraged to be as independent as possible. But younger children may need some help with personal skills such as using the toilet, dressing and eating. Older pupils may benefit from strategies to support and raise self-esteem through pastoral support and counselling. This may be helpful if a pupil loses a limb because of an accident or medical necessity, when it may be difficult to adjust emotionally. Adapted seating may be necessary and the use of a lift or stair lift to gain access to upper parts of the school building. If a pupil's writing speed is affected by the loss of a limb, the school can apply for extra time to be allowed in examinations such as the General Certificate of Secondary Education (GCSE).

Epilepsy

Epilepsy is a neurological condition typified by recurring seizures, that is, sudden episodes of uncontrolled electrical activity in the brain. These are associated with convulsions (violent movements of the limbs or body caused by muscular contractions), muscle spasms, involuntary movements and changes in perception and consciousness.

Engel (2001) outlines a diagnostic scheme. Seizures may be classified as: partial (affecting only one lobe or part of one side of the brain); and generalised (affecting the whole brain). Partial seizures are further classified as 'simple partial' or 'complex partial'. In simple partial seizures, the child remains conscious and may experience a tingling feeling in the arms or legs, disturbance of feeling, or disturbance of senses or perception (for example, the sense of smell may be affected). In complex partial seizures, consciousness is impaired but not completely lost. Behaviour may be confused and the child may be unresponsive. He may walk aimlessly or make staccato movements such as plucking at his clothes. Some of these behaviours may be misinterpreted as behavioural, emotional and social difficulties. Complex partial seizures can in seconds generalise to the whole brain, when they are described as 'complex partial with secondary generalisation'.

Generalised seizures are further classified as:

- *Tonic.* The body goes stiff and the child falls but does not have convulsions.
- *Clonic.* This involves spasms with muscles alternately contracting and relaxing.
- *Tonic-clonic.* The body stiffens and falls and then there are convulsions. The child may cry out, there may be saliva round the mouth and the child may lose bladder or bowel control.
- *Atonic.* The child falls limply to the floor.

◆ *Absence*. An absence seizure may be mistaken for loss of concentration. The child may stare into space with his eyelids flickering.
◆ *Myoclonus*. This is typified by brief jerking of a part of the body.
◆ *Unclassified*. This does not follow the typical pattern of other seizures.

(For fuller details of classification, see Appleton and Gibbs, 1998.)

Epilepsy is also classified according to an epilepsy syndrome where this can be done (about 60 per cent of cases). Among the implications of this for education is that it can help the parent and the teacher better understand the implications for learning, language and cognition that typify some of these classifications. Briefly, the classification involves an anatomical aspect, such as whether the epilepsy is localised or generalised, and aetiology (see Johnson and Parkinson, 2002, p. 9).

Causal factors relating to epilepsy are complex. The condition can occur as a result of an accident or head injury that may be followed by brain haemorrhage. Other causal factors are brain infections such as meningitis or encephalitis; or infections that cause abscesses that grow on the brain. Lack of oxygen at birth can cause brain damage leading later to epilepsy. Genetic factors appear to be implicated for some types of epilepsy; for example, in some instances, photo-sensitive epilepsy appears to have a genetic component (2002, pp. 3–4, 19).

A frequently quoted prevalence figure for epilepsy is that it affects 0.7 to 0.8 per cent of all school children aged 5 to 17 years in the United Kingdom (Appleton and Gibbs, 1998). However, about a third of all epilepsies beginning in childhood will apparently disappear by the start of adolescence (Johnson and Parkinson, 2002, p. 2)

The teacher needs to know such information as whether there are arrangements for tablets to be taken during the day; whether any side effects of medication are expected; and any changes in medication and their implications for school activities. In school, all incidences of seizures should be recorded and there are seizure description forms to assist this.

There are basic procedures that are followed if a child has a seizure (see, for example, Johnson and Parkinson, 2000, pp. 12 and 16). Certain procedures should be followed for tonic-clonic seizures, such as not moving the child unless he is in danger. Very occasionally there are emergencies requiring specific responses. For example, where the seizure does not look as though it is stopping after several minutes or the child has several seizures within a few minutes ('status epilepticus'), Valium may need to be administered rectally. This procedure is only followed by trained staff, with parental consent, and within guidelines and procedures agreed with the head teacher and the staff. Where a pupil has regular tonic-clonic fits, he may wear a helmet to protect his head.

It has been suggested that a teacher teaching a child with epilepsy should find out the type of seizures that the child experiences; their frequency and whether they occur at certain times; potential 'triggers' such as fatigue; and how the seizure should be dealt with should it occur (Johnson and Parkinson, 2002, p. 7). The ability to deal with seizures when they occur and to carefully record the progress of the seizure later is important as this has implications for the management of medication and other matters. Epilepsy can be associated with difficulties in:

- ◆ acquisition (taking in of information) especially if this is presented in chunks;
- ◆ retention, processing, categorising and prioritising of the assimilated information;
- ◆ formulation and expression (verbal and written) of an appropriate answer.

(pp. 59–60)

It is noted that 'Providing a structured framework, a routine in which to locate the information, helps to anchor the student in what can appear to be a frustrating and sometimes fragmentary process of information processing' (p. 60).

To help to ensure that information is assimilated, the teacher can:

- ◆ present information in short chunks;
- ◆ reinforce verbal information with written notes or bullet-pointed hand-outs;
- ◆ offer direct support when a pupil is felt to have difficulty in maintaining a focus of attention – particularly when working in group settings.

(p. 60)

In terms of behavioural, emotional and social development, pupils may feel frustrated and have low self-esteem because of the condition. The pastoral system may include opportunities for counselling and other provision to help. The potential embarrassment if a child with tonic-clonic seizures loses bladder or bowel control may be eased if the school plans ahead, for example by seeking to ensure privacy and keeping a second supply of the child's clothing.

Risk assessments are undertaken for some activities such as practical subjects, laboratory-based work and aspects of physical education to determine the balance between seeking to offer the pupil with epilepsy the widest curriculum opportunities and ensuring that he is safe.

Cystic fibrosis

'Cystic' refers to cysts, while 'fibrosis' is an overgrowth of scar or connective tissue. Cystic fibrosis, which occurs in about 1 in every 2,500 live births, is a life-threatening inherited disease present from birth in which thick mucus is produced on the lungs and the pancreas, resulting in cysts. The mucus causes lung infections and stops enzymes, which digest food, flowing from the pancreas to the intestines. In a very few instances cystic fibrosis is associated with other conditions such as a heart condition, cirrhosis of the liver, sinusitis, hay fever, arthritis and diabetes. Symptoms may be a persistent non-infectious cough, wheezing, lack of weight gain, and chest infections. The sexual maturity of a boy with the condition may be delayed and the average lifespan of a person with cystic fibrosis is about 30 years.

To alleviate digestive problems, a child may take a substance called pancreatin with meals to replace missing enzymes, helping food to be absorbed. Children with cystic fibrosis have to take enzymes with their food. Older pupils may need to take intravenous equipment with them about the school. Sometimes the child may need a nebuliser or may be prescribed a course of antibiotics to help clear an infection. Daily physiotherapy and breathing exercises are necessary to clear the child's lungs and, while this is often done before and after school, it may be necessary also in school time. A suitably trained learning support assistant may carry this out. Where pupils need intravenous treatment, arrangements are made between the head teacher, parents and school staff prepared to supervise. In general, school staff will need to liaise with others, such as the GP and the physiotherapist, to ensure that the treatment plans are fulfilled.

Pupils with cystic fibrosis should be able to participate in all school activities, but time may need to be allocated for physiotherapy as necessary. Learning and progress can be affected where the pupil needs frequent hospital care, although hospital schools provide education for pupils who may be in hospital for long periods. Also the school can be flexible in providing work if the pupil is at home and by allowing the pupil time to catch up on any missed work.

With regard to personal, social and health development, younger pupils, or those who require help, may need supervision at mealtimes to ensure that they eat well and remember to take any medication and food supplement capsules. Pupils may need additional pastoral support to help them deal with the frustrations to which the condition may give rise. Some pupils may have behavioural, emotional and social difficulties related to their capacity to cope with the condition. Suitable and sensitive behaviour management strategies are used if there are any behaviour difficulties. Teachers also need to be aware that pupils with cystic fibrosis may be teased about their coughing, small stature and need to take tablets with food (Hull Learning Services, 2004b, p. 18). Counselling can help teenagers to recognise and deal with the stress associated with delayed sexual maturity or other matters. Special arrangements may be made for GCSE examinations including allowing extra time, supervised breaks, or permission to take the examination in hospital or at home.

Asthma

Asthma, one of the most chronic childhood illnesses, is a physical condition causing the airways of the lungs to narrow, making breathing difficult. The sudden narrowing of the airways brings about an asthma attack. Allergies, exercise, stress, cold weather, viral infections and fumes such as those from vehicle exhausts or paint may precipitate asthma. Symptoms may include breathlessness, wheezing, repeated coughing, tightening of the chest and difficulty in breathing.

About 1 in 10 children experience asthma and it is estimated that, in the United Kingdom, it affects about 150,000 children.

Asthma is managed through taking steps to prevent it or in relieving it when symptoms appear. Medication that helps prevent asthma includes Intal or low dose steroids so long as these are taken regularly. Symptoms are relieved by medication such as Ventolin or Bricanyl. In extreme cases, a short course of steroid tablets may be prescribed. At school, staff should be aware of the symptoms of asthma and of what to do if an attack occurs. If a pupil is known to develop symptoms as a result of exercise, they should use their inhaler before the period of exercise. Should an attack occur, the pupil should rest before they restart an activity and should be reassured and calmed down. If the symptoms persist or become worse, medical attention should be summoned and, in severe cases, an ambulance should be called.

Pupils with asthma can attain similarly to children without the condition. But where asthma is not managed well, this can lead to frequent absences from school and the pupil can fall behind in his work. The school should develop the flexibility to enable the pupil to catch up with missed work, for example by rescheduling homework, providing summary notes of lessons and by support in homework clubs (see also Hull Learning Services, 2004c, p. 13).

Regarding PSHE, there should be pastoral care opportunities for the pupil with asthma to talk about any frustrations they may feel because of the condition and this should be supplemented by further support as necessary. The pupil should be encouraged to use medication independently and responsibly to avoid attacks.

Participation in sports and other physical education activities may be restricted, especially if they are outdoors in cold weather. Short periods of exercise are less likely to bring on an attack than long ones, having obvious implications for the management of physical education lessons.

Diabetes mellitus (type 1)

The type of diabetes described here is diabetes mellitus, caused by the pancreas not producing (or producing insufficient amounts of) the hormone insulin. Insulin enables glucose to be absorbed into cells for their energy needs and the liver and fat cells for storage. If there is not enough insulin, the levels of glucose in the blood become too high, causing extreme thirst and the passing of excessive amounts of urine. Because the body is unable to store the glucose, this causes tiredness and hunger and can lead to loss of weight.

The two types of diabetes mellitus are type 1 (the insulin dependent type) and type 2 (the non-insulin dependent type). Type 1 is the more severe and usually appears between the ages of 10 and 16 years. The insulin-producing cells in the pancreas are destroyed, and the production of insulin stops almost completely so that regular injections of insulin are needed. Type 2 usually develops in people over the age of 40 years.

While diabetes mellitus tends to run in families, only a small percentage of those inheriting the genes responsible for the insulin dependent form eventually develop the disease, when it is thought to be the delayed result of an earlier viral infection. Obesity, particular illnesses, certain drugs, infections and pregnancy may precipitate latent diabetes.

Diabetes mellitus type 1 is treated in two ways. The person injects him or herself with insulin between one and four times a day. Also, a diet is followed, which regulates the intake of carbohydrates and ensures that their intake is spread out during the day. This avoids marked fluctuations in the levels of glucose in the blood. Too much glucose leads to symptoms of the untreated disease. Too little can cause weakness, sweating, confusion and even seizures and unconsciousness. The blood and urine levels of glucose are regularly self-monitored using a do-it-yourself test kit. Teachers need to be aware of the medical and dietary requirements of a child with diabetes and should receive training in noticing possible signs of glucose imbalance, taking appropriate action and summoning medical assistance as necessary.

In personal, social and health development, the child needs to be encouraged and supported as necessary in ensuring the proper monitoring and treatment of glucose levels. Dietary requirements should be strictly adhered to.

Approaches and provision and their educational importance

It will be noticed that some disabilities and medical conditions are associated with particular provision. Also, there are broader observations that may be made with regard to education.

While medical conditions do not necessarily imply SEN, it is necessary for effective education, including any special educational provision, to take place so that the child and others effectively manage medical conditions. The child's educational provision has to be responsive to changes in the physical and motor abilities of the child and sensitive to the physical, psychological and any other effects of the medical condition.

With conditions associated with physical and motor disability, similarly, medical requirements have to be provided for. Difficulties with physical abilities and mobility are aided through various means, including adaptations to the environment; flexibility in routines; particular emphases in the curriculum, including PSHCE; the use of equipment and aids; the support of a learning support assistant; speech and language therapy; and programmes to develop and consolidate motor skills, including physiotherapy and motor training.

As an example of a specific approach, conductive education is a form of education for children with motor difficulties, such as those associated with cerebral palsy, multiple sclerosis and head injuries. Its aim is 'orthofunction' – the ability to carry out functional movements independently. Specially trained staff known as 'conductors' provide conductive education and two or more usually work through the day with a small group of children in a residential setting. The conductor teaches the child skills such as walking and feeding and also teaches reading and number. So that they can take over when the child leaves the institution, parents are involved from an early stage. Reservations have been expressed about conductive education in that some comparative studies have indicated that it is less effective than conventional methods of teaching and therapy used in special schools in the United Kingdom. However, it is possible that some of the principles of conductive education can inform approaches to motor development and the strengths of the approach can be identified and developed in a way that is not too rigid. The Treloar School, Hampshire, for example, uses an adapted form of conductive education.

THINKING POINTS

Readers may wish to consider:

♦   how best to ensure the support at the LEA level and the whole school level that is necessary to effectively educate pupils with the conditions discussed;

♦ what training will be needed in relation to this and how it can be ensured that it is up to date;

♦ the broad and common features of provision for many pupils with physical or motor disabilities, such as wheelchair access and flexible starting and finishing times to lessons;

♦ the provision that is more specific to particular conditions, such as counselling and pastoral support relating to reduced life expectancy in certain conditions such as multiple sclerosis;

♦ the importance of personal, social and health development and raising self-esteem for many pupils with physical and motor disabilities.

KEY TEXTS

Hull Learning Services (2004b) *Supporting Children with Medical Conditions*, London, David Fulton Publishers.

Section one of the book concerns medical conditions and possible educational implications; section two considers 'meeting the pupil's physical needs'; section three deals with access to the curriculum; and section four looks at 'developing skills for learning'.

Pickles, P. A. C. (2004) *Inclusive Teaching, Inclusive Learning: Managing the Curriculum for Children with Severe Motor Difficulties*, 2nd edn, London, David Fulton Publishers.

This provides practical suggestions for those working with children having severe motor difficulties. Due emphasis is given to the importance of joint professional working, the use of equipment, and approaches within particular curriculum areas. Information is provided on the Communication and Aids Project, which runs until 2006.

Chapter 6

Conclusion

In this brief concluding chapter, I suggest differences and common features of sensory impairments and physical disabilities; and look at possible ways of evaluating provision.

Differences and common features

When examining the approaches used in the education of pupils with visual impairment and pupils having hearing impairment, common features are that both are sensory impairments of crucial 'distance senses'. But differences are important for education, with communication being a central feature of the education of deaf children and low vision aids and tactile modes of learning being essential for the education of children with visual impairment.

In educating pupils who are deafblind, again there are areas that are common with pupils having visual impairment, such as that the best use is made of any residual vision. Approaches shared with pupils who are deafblind and pupils who have hearing impairment include ensuring that there is an optimum listening environment. For teachers working with pupils who have visual impairments, hearing impairment or who are deafblind, another aspect of provision is the importance of making sure that their knowledge and skills at least reach the standards required by the 'teachers with specialist skills' standards (Teacher Training Agency, 1999) and liaising closely with specialist teachers having mandatory qualifications.

But, beyond such areas, it is the differences between the provision for pupils who are deafblind and pupils who have either a visual or a hearing impairment that are noticeable and important. It is often mentioned that deafblindness is more than deafness plus blindness, and this is one of the reasons that criteria for deafblindness may accept higher sensory thresholds than for deafness and blindness separately. Educational implications include the particular focus on sensory and manual work including communication.

Turning to physical disability and medical conditions, certain implications may often be common to different types of disability or medical condition. Where the pupil has difficulties with mobility, features such as considering flexibility of the start and finish times of school lessons are helpful generally, as are the arrangement of furniture and the use of particular aids within each classroom. Other aspects that are common to provision for many pupils with physical disabilities include: improving physical access and mobility; providing as necessary for other SEN that may be evident, such as visual impairment or learning difficulties; and raising self-esteem through such means as counselling and pastoral care. Yet others are: differentiating the curriculum and learning through appropriate means including as necessary support staff, augmented communication aids and adaptive equipment; ensuring timely support from various services; and making sure medical procedures are understood and followed and supporting this by regularly updated staff training. Where pupils have to spend time away from school because of illness, support and flexibility in providing work is necessary.

Differences in the types of physical disability can be important educationally; for example, particular care is taken with loss of attention for pupils with epilepsy, while for a pupil with cerebral palsy movement skills are a particular focus of the curriculum.

Evaluating provision

A general justification of educational provision is likely to have two elements, one explanatory and one pragmatic. First, the intervention should look or sound as though it *ought* to work. It should be possible, indeed fairly easy, to explain it and why it works. For example, if a child is likely to have difficulty with mobility unaided, then interventions such as mobility training would naturally be expected to be useful and effective. If explanations require leaps of faith or are propagated by charismatic discoverers of a technique who consider close scrutiny damaging to the approach, practitioners and anyone else should exercise great caution. Similarly, if interventions relate to vague or unsubstantiated hypotheses about brain activity or are wrapped in impenetrable jargon, considerable care is required. The book, *Controversial Issues in Special Education* by Gary Hornby and his colleagues (Hornby *et al.*, 1998), forms a sobering corrective for anyone tempted by 'fad' treatments or for that matter fad 'diagnoses'.

Second, there should be evidence that the approach or intervention *has* worked. Reading about an approach and then visiting a special school, unit, mainstream school or other venue where it is being used and is working provides useful information for the teacher and others. One needs to be clear about what the expression 'an approach is working' means. Is the intervention teaching the child skills or knowledge that are deemed necessary? Is it enabling learning to take place more effectively? It is also important to consider the extent to which an approach that appears to be successful in one venue can be applied to another venue with other children. An important question is 'Is it important that the children with whom it is proposed to introduce a new intervention are similar (e.g. in age or cognitive level) to those with whom the approach is working successfully?'

Progress and achievement and attainment will indicate the success of interventions as they demonstrate the success of education for all children. Achievement is understood in broad terms to include progress in personal, emotional and social development. As approaches are used, the school will continually monitor and evaluate the effect on pupils' progress, achievement and attainment and refine and improve, or change, approaches accordingly.

Addresses

Association for Dance Movement Therapy UK
32 Meadfoot Lane
Torquay
Devon TQ1 2BW

e-mail: queries@admt.org.uk
www.admt.org.uk

> ADMTUK involves a national network of sub-committees. Its work includes quarterly workshops, conferences and seminars; professional registration; education and training; and publications such as *e-motion* and research.

The Association of Educational Psychologists
26 The Avenue
Durham DH1 4ED

Tel: 0191 384 9512
Fax: 0191 386 5287
e-mail: aep@aep.org.uk
www.aep.org.uk

> The AEP is the professional association for educational psychologists in England and Wales and Northern Ireland.

The Association of Professional Music Therapists
61 Church Hill Road
East Barnet
Herts EN4 8SY

Tel/fax: 020 8440 4153
e-mail: APMToffice@aol.com
www.apmt.org

The APMT supports and develops the profession of music therapy. Its members are qualified music therapists who have taken a recognised post-graduate training course in music therapy. The association aims to maintain high standards of practice through administering and monitoring a range of professional development schemes.

The British Association of Art Therapists
The Claremont Project
24–7 White Lion Street
London N1 9PD

Tel: 020 7686 4216
Fax: 020 7837 7945
e-mail: info@baat.org
www.baat.org

The BAAT provides information to its members and to the public concerning all aspects of art therapy. It publishes a journal, *Inscape*, and oversees stand-ards of training and professional practice.

The British Association of Play Therapists
31 Cedar Drive
Keynsham
Bristol BS31 2TY

Tel/fax: 01179 860 390
e-mail: info@bapt.uk.com
www.bapt.info

The Association provides a support network for play therapists and informa-tion on training courses.

British Educational Communications and Technology Agency (BECTA)
Millburn Hill Road
Science Park
Coventry CV4 7JJ

Tel: 0247 641 6994
e-mail: communications@becta.org.uk
www.becta.org.uk

A UK-wide agency supporting UK education departments in their strategic ICT developments.

British Psychological Society
St Andrew's House
48 Princess Road East
Leicester LE1 7DR

Tel: 0116 254 9568
Fax: 0116 247 0787
e-mail: bps1@le.ac.uk
www.bps.org.uk

The BPS is the professional body for psychologists in the United Kingdom, having various sub-groups and divisions. It publishes the monthly magazine *Psychologist*, which is of generic interest to psychologists. Its specialist journals include *The British Journal of Clinical Psychology* and *The British Journal of Educational Psychology*.

The British Society for Music Therapy
61 Churchill Road
East Barnet
Hertfordshire EN4 8SL

Tel: 020 8441 6226
Fax: 020 8441 4118
e-mail: info@bsmt.org
www.bsmt.org

The BSMT organises courses, conferences, workshops and meetings concerning music therapy, which are open to all. An information booklet giving details of music therapy, training courses, books and meetings is available to enquirers. The BSMT has its own publications and offers music therapy books for sale. Members receive *The British Journal of Music Therapy* and the *BSMT Bulletin*.

Cruse Bereavement Care
Cruse House
126 Sheen Road
Richmond TW9 1UR

Tel: 020 8939 9530
e-mail: info@crusebereavementcare.org.uk
www.crusebereavementcare.org.uk

A charity specialising in bereavement care.

The Fragile X Society
53 Winchelsea Lane
Hastings
East Sussex TN35 4LG

Tel: 01424 813 147
e-mail: lesleywalker@fragilex.k-web.co.uk
www.fragilex.org.uk

Genetic Interest Group
Unit 4D
Leroy House
436 Essex Road
London N1 3QP

Tel: 020 7704 3141
Fax: 020 7359 1447
e-mail: mail@gig.org.uk
www.gig.org.uk

Harcourt Assessment (The Psychological Corporation)
Halley Court
Jordan Hill
Oxford OX2 8EJ

Tel: 01865 888 188
Fax: 01865 314 348
e-mail: info@harcourt-uk.com
www.harcourt-uk.com

The National Institute of Conductive Education
Cannon Hill House
Russell Road
Moseley
Birmingham B13 8RG

Tel: 0121 449 1569
Fax: 0121 449 1611
e-mail: foundation@conductive-education.org.uk
www.conductive-education.org.uk

NFER-Nelson
The Chiswick Centre
414 Chiswick High Road
London W4 5TF

Tel: 020 8996 8444
Fax: 020 8996 5358
e-mail: edu&hsc@nfer-Nelson.co.uk
www.nfer-nelson.co.uk

NFER-Nelson are test suppliers whose tests include ones relevant to BESD.

Partnership for Children
26–7 Market Place
Kingston-upon-Thames
Surrey KT1 1JH

Tel: 020 8974 6004
Fax: 020 8974 6600
e-mail: info@partnershipforchildren.org.uk
www.partnershipforchildren.org.uk

Royal National Institute for the Blind (RNIB)
105 Judd Street
London WC1H 9NE

Tel: 020 7388 1266
e-mail: helpline@rnib.org.uk
www.rnib.org.uk

A national charity supporting people with visual problems, their families and professionals.

Royal National Institute for the Deaf (RNID)
19–23 Featherstone Street
London EC1Y 8SL

Tel: 0808 808 0123
e-mail: informationline@rnid.org.uk
www.rnid.org.uk

A national charity providing an information line, a help line, advice, specialist information research and other services.

The Signalong Group
Stratford House
Waterside Court
Neptune Way
Rochester
Kent ME2 4NZ

Tel: 0870 774 3752
Fax: 0870 744 3758
e-mail: mkennard@signalong.org.uk
www.signalong.org.uk

Soundbeam
Unit 3
Highbury Villas
St Michael's Hill
Bristol BS2 8BY

Tel: 0117 974 4142
Fax: 0117 970 6241
e-mail: tim@soundbeam.co.uk
www.soundbeam.co.uk

Widgit Software
124 Cambridge Science Park
Milton Road
Cambridge CB4 0ZS

Tel: 01223 425 558
Fax: 01223 425 349
e-mail: info@widgit.com
www.widgit.com

Bibliography

Aitken, S. (1995) 'Assessment of deafblind learners', in Etheridge, D. (ed.) *The Education of Dual Sensory Impaired Children: Recognising and Developing Ability*, London, David Fulton Publishers.

—— (2000) 'Understanding deaf blindness', in Aitken, S., Buultjens, M., Clark, C. *et al.* (eds) *Teaching Children Who Are Deafblind: Contact Communication and Learning*, London, David Fulton Publishers: 1–34.

—— and Buultjens, M. (1992) *Vision for Doing: Assessing Functional Vision of Learners who are Multiply Disabled*, Edinburgh, Moray House.

—— and Millar, S. (2002) *Listening to Children with Communication Support Needs*, Glasgow, Sense Scotland.

——, Buultjens, M., Clark, C. *et al.* (eds) (2000) *Teaching Children who are Deafblind: Contact, Communication and Learning*, London, David Fulton Publishers.

Aldrich, F. K. and Parkin, A. J. (1989) 'Listening at speed', *British Journal of Visual Impairment*, 7, 1: 16–18.

Appleton, R. and Gibbs, J. (1998) *Epilepsy in Childhood and Adolescence*, London, Dunitz.

Armitage, I. M., Burke, J. P. and Buffin, J. T. (1995) 'Visual impairment in severe and profound sensorineural deafness', *Archives of Diseases in Childhood*, 73: 53–6.

Arter, C. and Malin, K. (1997) 'Physical education', in Mason, H. and McCall, S. with Arter, C. *et al.* (eds) *Visual Impairment: Access to Education for Children and Young People*, London, David Fulton Publishers: 279–88.

——, McCall, S. and Bowyer, T. (1996) 'Handwriting and children with visual impairments', *British Journal of Special Education*, 23, 1: 25–9.

Baker, R. (1990) 'Developing literacy skills through dialogue journals', in *Bilingual Education for Deaf Children: From Policy to Practice*, Nottingham, Laser Conference Proceedings.

—— and Knight, P. (1998) '"Total Communication" – current policy and practice', in Gregory, S., Knight, P., McCracken, W. *et al.* (eds) *Issues in Deaf Education*, London, David Fulton Publishers.

Banks, J., Gray, P. and Fyfe, R. (1990) 'The written recall of printed stories by severely deaf children', *British Journal of Educational Psychology*, 60: 192–206.

Bellugi, U., O'Grady, L., Lillo-Martin, M. *et al.* (1994) 'Enhancement of spatial cognition in deaf children', in Volterra, V. and Erting, C. (eds) *From Gesture to Language in Hearing and Deaf Children*, Washington, DC, Gallaudet University Press.

Best, A. (1997) 'Management issues in multiple disabilities', in Mason, H. and McCall, S. with Arter, C. *et al.* (eds) *Visual Impairment: Access to Education for Children and Young People*, London, David Fulton Publishers: 377–85.

Best, A. B. (1992) *Teaching Children with Visual Impairments*, Milton Keynes, Open University Press.

Blum, P. (2004) *Improving Low Reading Ages in the Secondary School: Practical Strategies for Learning Support*, London, RoutledgeFalmer.

Booth, T. and Ainscow, M. with Black-Hawkins, K. (2000) *Index for Inclusion*, Bristol, Centre for Studies in Inclusive Education.

Braden, J. P. (1994) *Deafness, Deprivation and IQ*, London, Plenum Press.

Bradley, H. (1991) *Assessing Communication Together*, Penarth, Mental Health Nurses Association.

Braille Authority of the United Kingdom (1987) *Braille Mathematics Notation*, London, RNIB.

British Deaf Association (1996) *The Right to be Equal: British Deaf Association Education Policy*, London, BDA.

Campbell, R. and Wright, H. (1990) 'Deafness and immediate memory for pictures: dissociations between "inner speech" and the "inner ear"', *Journal of Experimental Child Psychology*, 50: 259–86.

Chapman, E. K., Tobin, M. J., Tooze, F. H. *et al.* (1989) *Look and Think: A Handbook for Teachers: Visual Perception Training for Visually Impaired Children (5–11 years)*, 2nd revised edn, London, RNIB.

Clark, C. (2000) 'Personal and social development', in Aitken, S., Buultjens, M., Clark, C. *et al.* (eds) *Teaching Children who are Deafblind: Contact, Communication and Learning*, London, David Fulton Publishers: 83–118.

Clunies-Ross, L. and Franklin, A. (1996) *RNIB Survey of LEAs: Educational Placement of Children who are VI or MDVI in England, Wales and Scotland*, London, RNIB.

Coupe, J., Barton, L., Barber, M. *et al.* (1985) *The Affective Communication Assessment*, Manchester, Manchester Education Committee.

DAHISS (1996) *English as a Foreign Language Curriculum*, Leeds, Leeds Deaf and Hearing Impaired Support Services.

Deaf-Blind Services Liaison Group (1988) *Breaking Through: Developing Services for Deaf-Blind People*, London, SENSE (National Deaf-Blind Rubella Association).

Deaf Education Through Listening and Talking (DELTA) (1997) *The Right to Hear and be Heard: Raising Standards in the Education of Deaf Children*, Haverhill, DELTA.

Denton, D. (1976) 'The philosophy of total communication', *Supplement to British Deaf News*, Carlisle, British Deaf Association.

Department for Education and Skills (2001a) *Special Educational Needs Code of Practice*, London, DfES.

—— (2001b) *Inclusive Schooling: Children with Special Educational Needs*, London, DfES.

—— (2001c) *Access to Education for Children and Young People with Medical Needs*, London, DfES.

—— (2003) *Data Collection by Type of Special Educational Needs*, London, DfES.

—— (2004) *National Statistics First Release: Special Educational Needs in England*, January (SFR 44/2004), London, DfES.

Dorton House School for the Blind (1995) *Braille Mathematics Notation – A Simplified Version*, London, Royal London Society for the Blind.

Elliot, C. D. (2005) *British Ability Scales*, 2nd edn, Windsor, NFER-Nelson.

Engel, J. (2001) 'ILAE Commission report: a proposed diagnostic scheme for people with epileptic seizures and with epilepsy. Report of the ILAE task force on classification and terminology', *Epilepsia*, 42, 6: 1–8.

Eyre, J. T. (2000) 'Holistic assessment', in Aitken, S., Buultjens, M., Clark, C. *et al.* (eds) *Teaching Children Who Are Deafblind: Contact, Communication and Learning*, London, David Fulton Publishers: 119–40.

Farrell, M. (2000) 'Educational inclusion and raising standards', *British Journal of Special Education*, 21, 1: 35–8.

—— (2003) *The Special Education Handbook*, London, David Fulton Publishers.

Fortnum, H., Davies, A., Butler, A. *et al.* (1996) *Health Service Implications of Changes in Aetiology and Referral Patterns of Hearing Impaired Children in Trent 1985–93 – Report to Trent Health*, Nottingham and Sheffield, Medical Research Council Institute of Hearing Research and Trent Health.

Gallaway, C. and Young, A. (2003) (eds) *Deafness and Education in the UK – Research Perspectives*, London, Whurr Publishers.

Gartner, A. and Lipsky, D. K. (1989) 'New conceptualisations for special education', *European Journal of Special Needs Education*, 4, 1: 16–21.

Greaney, J., Arter, C., Hill, E. *et al.* (1994) 'The development of a new test of children's braille-reading ability', *British Journal of Visual Impairment*, 15, 1: 10–14.

Greenwood, C. (2002) *Understanding the Needs of Parents: Guidelines for Effective Collaboration with Parents of Children with Special Educational Needs*, London, David Fulton Publishers.

Gregory, S. and Pickersgill, M. (1997) 'Towards a model of bilingual education for deaf children', *Laserbeam*, Spring, 28: 3–8.

——, Knight, P., McCracken, W. *et al.* (eds) (1998) *Issues in Deaf Education*, London, David Fulton Publishers.

Griffiths, J. and Best, A. (1996) *Survey of Visually Impaired Children in Schools for Children with Severe Learning Difficulties*, Condover, RNIB Condover Hall School.

Hewett, D. and Nind, M. (eds) (1998) *Interaction in Action: Reflections on the Use of Intensive Interaction*, London, David Fulton Publishers.

Hodges, L. (2000) 'Effective teaching and learning', in Aitken, S., Buultjens, M., Clark, C. *et al.* (eds) *Teaching Children Who Are Deafblind: Contact, Communication and Learning*, London, David Fulton Publishers: 167–99.

Hornby, G. (2003) 'Counselling and guidance of parents', in Hornby, G. Hall, E. and Hall, C. (eds) *Counselling Pupils in Schools: Skills and Strategies for Teachers*, London, RoutledgeFalmer: 129–40.

——, Atkinson, M. and Howard, J. (1998) *Controversial Issues in Special Education*, London, David Fulton Publishers.

Hull, T. and Mason, H. L. (1993) 'The speed of information processing test for the blind in a tactile version', *British Journal of Visual Impairment*, 11, 1: 21–3.

Hull Learning Services (2004a) *Supporting Children with Cerebral Palsy*, London, David Fulton Publishers.

—— (2004b) *Supporting Children with Medical Conditions*, London, David Fulton Publishers.

—— (2004c) *Supporting Children with Asthma*, London, David Fulton Publishers.

Johnson, M. and Parkinson, G. (2002) *Epilepsy: A Practical Guide*, London, David Fulton Publishers.

Keil, S. and Clunies-Ross, L. (2003) *Survey of Educational Provision for Blind and Partially Sighted Children in England, Scotland and Wales*, London, Royal National Institute for the Blind, Education and Employment Research Department.

Kenward, H. (1997) *Integrating Pupils with Disabilities in Mainstream Schools*, London, David Fulton Publishers.

Kiernan, C. and Reid, B. (1987) *Pre-verbal Communication Schedule*, Windsor, NFER-Nelson.

Kingsley, M. (1997) 'The effects of visual loss', in Mason, H. and McCall, S. with Arter, C. *et al.* (eds) (1997) *Visual Impairment: Access to Education for Children and Young People*, London, David Fulton Publishers: 23–9.

Kirkwood, R. and McCall, S. (1997) 'Educational provision', in Mason, H., and McCall, S. with Arter, C. *et al.* (eds) *Visual Impairment: Access to Education for Children and Young People*, London, David Fulton Publishers: 13–20.

Knight, P. and Swanwick, R. (2002) *Working with Deaf Pupils: Sign Bilingual Policy into Practice*, London, David Fulton Publishers.

Leeds Local Education Authority (1995) *Deaf and Hearing Impaired Support Services (DAHISS) Policy Statement*, Leeds, LEA Publications.

Lewis, A. (2004) 'And when did you last see your father? Exploring the views of children with learning difficulties/disabilities', *British Journal of Special Education*, 31, 1: 3–9.

Lewis, S. (1996) 'The reading achievements of a group of severely and profoundly hearing impaired school leavers educated within a natural oral approach', *Journal of the British Association of Teachers of the Deaf*, 20, 1: 1–7.

—— (1998) 'Reading and writing within an oral/aural approach', in Gregory, S., Knight, P., McCracken, W. *et al.* (eds) *Issues in Deaf Education*, London, David Fulton Publishers.

Logan, K., Mayberry, M. and Fletcher, J. (1996) 'The short term memory of profoundly deaf people for words, signs and abstract spatial stimuli', *Applied Cognitive Psychology*, 10: 105–19.

McCall, S. (1997) 'The development of literacy through touch', in Mason, H. and McCall, S. with Arter, C. *et al.* (eds) *Visual Impairment: Access to Education for Children and Young People*, London, David Fulton Publishers.

—— and McLinden, M. (1996) 'Literacy: a foot in the door', *Eye Contact*, 16, Autumn (supplement): 149–58.

McCracken, W. (1998a) 'Introduction' (to section 4, Audiology), in Gregory, S., Knight, P., McCracken, W. *et al.* (eds) *Issues in Deaf Education*, London, David Fulton Publishers: 155–6.

—— (1998b) 'Deaf children with disabilities', in Gregory, S., Knight, P., McCracken, W. *et al.* (eds) *Issues in Deaf Education*, London, David Fulton Publishers: 28–37.

McLinden, M. (1997) 'Children with multiple disabilities and a visual impairment', in Mason, H. and McCall, S. with Arter, C. *et al.* (eds) *Visual Impairment: Access to Education for Children and Young People*, London, David Fulton Publishers: 313–23.

McSweeney, M. (1998) 'Cognition and deafness', in Gregory, S., Knight, P., McCracken, W. *et al.* (eds) *Issues in Deaf Education*, London, David Fulton Publishers: 20–7.

Maltby, M. T. and Knight, P. (2001) *Audiology: An Introduction for Teachers and Other Professionals*, London, David Fulton Publishers.

Marchant, R. and Cross, M. (2002) *How It Is*, London, National Society for the Prevention of Cruelty to Children.

Marcotte, A. C. and Morere, D. A. (1990) 'Speech lateralisation in deaf populations: evidence for a developmental critical period', *Journal of Brain and Language*, 39: 134–52.

Mason, H. and McCall, S. with Arter, C. *et al.* (eds) (1997) *Visual Impairment: Access to Education for Children and Young People*, London, David Fulton Publishers.

Maxwell, M. (1992) 'Simultaneous communication: the state of the art and proposals for change', in Stokoe, W. (ed.) *Simultaneous Communication, ASL and Other Classroom Communication Modes*, Burtonsville, MD, Linstok Press.

Murdoch, H. (1997) 'Multi-sensory impairment', in Mason, H. and McCall, S. with Arter, C. *et al.* (eds) *Visual Impairment: Access to Education for Children and Young People*, London, David Fulton Publishers: 355–65.

Nafstad, A. (2000) 'Co-creating communication', in *NUD Newsletter*, Winter 2000, Dronninglund, Nordic Staff Development Centre.

—— and Rødbroe, I. (1999) *Co-creating Communication*, Oslo, Forlaget-Nord Press.

National Deaf Children's Society (1996) *NDCS Directory 1996–7*, London, NDCS.

Neville, H. J., Coffey, S. A., Lawson, D. S. *et al.* (1997) 'Neural systems mediating American sign language: effects of sensory experience and age of acquisition', *Brain and Language*, 57: 285–308.

Nind, M. (1996) 'Efficacy of intensive interaction: developing sociability and communication in people with severe and complex learning difficulties using an approach based on caregiver–infant interaction', *European Journal of Special Needs Education*, 11: 1.

—— and Hewett, D. (1994) *Access to Communication*, London, David Fulton Publishers.

—— and —— (2001) *A Practical Guide to Intensive Interaction*, Kidderminster, British Institute of Learning Difficulties.

Nunes, T. and Moreno, C. (1997a) 'Is hearing impairment a cause of difficulty in learning mathematics?', *Report to the Nuffield Foundation*.

—— and —— (1997b) 'Solving problems with different ways of representing the task: how do deaf children perform?', *Equals* 3, 2: 15–17.

Orelove, F. P. and Sobsey, D. (1991) *Educating Children with Multiple Disabilities: A Transdisciplinary Approach*, Baltimore, MD, Paul H. Brookes.

Partridge, S. (1996) 'Video stories for 7–11s', in Galloway, C. (ed.) *Using Videos with Deaf Children*, Manchester, Centre for Audiology, Education of the Deaf and Speech Pathology, University of Manchester.

Pau, C. S. (1995) 'The deaf child and solving the problems of arithmetic', *American Annals of the Deaf*, 140, 3: 287–90.

Pease, L. (2000) 'Creating a communicating environment', in Aitken, S., Buultjens, M., Clark, C. *et al.* (eds) *Teaching Children who are Deafblind: Contact Communication and Learning*, London, David Fulton Publishers: 35–82.

Phoenix, S. (1988) *An Interim Report on a Pilot Survey of Deaf Adults in Northern Ireland*, Belfast, Northern Ireland Workshop with Deaf.

Pickersgill, M. (1998) 'Bilingualism – current policy and practice', in Gregory, S., Knight, P., McCracken, W. *et al.* (eds) *Issues in Deaf Education*, London, David Fulton Publishers: 88–97.

—— and Gregory, S. (1998) *Sign Bilingualism: A Model*, London, Adept Press.

Pickles, P. A. C. (2004) *Inclusive Teaching, Inclusive Learning: Managing the Curriculum for Children with Severe Motor Difficulties*, 2nd edn, London, David Fulton Publishers.

Poizner, H. and Tallal, P. (1987) 'Temporal processing in deaf signers', *Brain and Language*, 30: 52–62.

Porter, G. and Kirkland, J. (1995) *Integrating Alternative and Augmentative Communication into Group Programmes – Utilising the Principles of Conductive Education*, Australia, Spastics Society of Victoria.

Porter, J., Miller, O. and Pease, L. (1997) *Curriculum Access for Deafblind Children: Research Report No. 1*, London, Department for Education and Employment/ Sense.

Qualifications and Curriculum Authority (1999) *Shared World – Different Experiences: Designing the Curriculum for Pupils who are Deafblind*, London, QCA.

Ridgeway, S. (1998) 'A deaf personality', in Gregory, S., Knight, P., McCracken, W. *et al.* (eds) *Issues in Deaf Education*, London, David Fulton Publishers.

Sense (2002) *Quality Standards in Education Support Services for Children and Young People who are Deafblind/Multi-sensory Impaired*, London, Sense.

—— (2004) *Reaching Out: A Toolkit for Deafblind Children's Services*, London, Sense.

Stillman, R. (1978) *Callier Azusa Scale*, Austin, TX, University of Texas.

Stone, J. (1995) *Mobility for Special Needs*, London, Cassell.

—— (1997a) 'The pre-school child', in Mason, H. and McCall, S. with Arter, C. *et al.* (eds) *Visual Impairment: Access to Education for Children and Young People*, London, David Fulton Publishers. 87–96.

—— (1997b) 'Mobility and independence skills', in Mason, H. and McCall, S. with Arter, C. *et al.* (eds) *Visual Impairment: Access to Education for Children and Young People*, London, David Fulton Publishers: 159–68.

Swanwick, R. (1993) 'The use of DARTs to develop deaf children's literacy skills within a bilingual context', *Deafness and Development*, 3, 2: 4–9.

—— (1998) 'The teaching and learning of literacy within a sign bilingual approach', in Gregory, S., Knight, P., McCracken, W. *et al.* (eds) *Issues in Deaf Education*, London, David Fulton Publishers: 111–18.

—— (2003) 'Sign bilingual deaf children's writing strategies: responses to different sources for writing', in Galloway, C. and Young, A. (eds) *Deafness and Education in the UK – Research Perspectives*, London, Whurr Publishers.

Teacher Training Agency (1999) *National Special Educational Needs Specialist Standards*, London, TTA.

van Dijk, J. (1989) 'The Sint Michilsgestel approach to diagnosis and education of multi sensory impaired persons', in Best, A. B. (ed.) *Sensory Impairment with Multi-handicap: Current Philosophies and New Approaches*, A European Conference, Warwick University, 6–11 August 1989: Papers on the Education of the Deaf-Blind, International Association for the Education of the Deaf-Blind.

Wade, J. (1999) 'Including all learners: QCA's approach', *British Journal of Special Education*, 26, 2: 80–2.

Whittles, S. (1998) *Can You Hear Us?: Including the Views of Disabled Children and Young People*, London, Save the Children.

World Health Organization (1980) *International Classification of Impairments, Disabilities and Handicaps: A Manual of Classification Relating to the Consequences of Disease*, Geneva, WHO.

Index